BLOCKS, COINS, AND CONFIDENCE

A Personal Guide to the Crypto Space
by an Educator and Enthusiast

CHARLES E TYLER

📖 A Lifetime of Learning, Leading, and Lifting Others

For over 25 years, Charles has dedicated himself to education, leadership, and personal development. Whether he was standing at the front of a classroom, mentoring young professionals, or helping organizations adapt to change, his guiding principles have remained the same: clarity, compassion, and purpose-driven growth.

He holds a Bachelor of Science in Chemistry and Mathematics Education and a Master of Business Administration (MBA), a rare and powerful academic pairing that reflects his analytical mindset and business acumen. His background allows him to seamlessly bridge two worlds: the logical precision of STEM fields and the strategic thinking required in the business world.

Charles has received numerous leadership awards, teaching honors, and professional accolades throughout his career, recognizing his impact on academic excellence and leadership development. Whether in classrooms, universities, or professional settings, he is known for pairing high expectations with a thoughtful and personal approach. Those who have worked with him, including students, colleagues, and peers, often describe him as someone who builds confidence, inspires critical thinking, and mentors with genuine care.

🔐 Blockchain Credentials You Can Trust

In a space where credentials and education matter more than ever, Charles's certifications speak to the depth and breadth of his expertise. His standout blockchain, crypto, fintech, and compliance designations include:

- Certified Blockchain Expert (CBE™)
- Certified Web 3.0 Professional (CW3P™)
- Certified Crypto Expert (CCE™)

- Certified Enterprise Blockchain Professional (CEBP)
- Certified Metaverse Professional™ (CMP™)
- Certified Blockchain & KYC Professional™
- Certified Cryptocurrency Investigator™ (CCI — General, Ethereum, and Advanced tracks)
- Certified Cryptocurrency Auditor™ (CCA™)
- Certified Cryptocurrency Security Investigator
- Certified NFT Professional™ and Certified NFT Expert™
- Certified AI Professional (CAIP™)
- Certified Fintech Expert™ (CFTE™)
- DACFP Advanced Certificate in Blockchain & Digital Assets (CBDA) — Financial Advisor Track
- Crypto Compliance Advanced Certification
- Certified Blockchain Project Manager (CBPM)
- Global Blockchain Professional (GBP™)

Charles is known for sharing the reason behind pursuing such a wide range of certifications with one guiding principle: each of these credentials has sharpened his ability to teach others with clarity, accuracy, and ethics.

Together, these achievements reflect Charles's comprehensive and disciplined study of digital assets, from the technical mechanics of blockchain networks, token economies, and decentralized applications to the critical areas of security, compliance, financial crime prevention, and emerging technology ethics.

And yes, there are many more, because to Charles, learning isn't something you finish. It's a lifetime commitment.

🐢 An Educator on a Mission

At the core of everything Charles does is a simple but powerful truth: *Education is empowerment.*

When it's clear, honest, and accessible, education turns fear into confidence, confusion into clarity, and barriers into open doors.

Whether building a beginner-friendly blockchain course, helping a retiree understand how crypto wallets work, or talking to everyday folks about digital assets, Charles shows up with the same purpose: to make knowledge a bridge, not a wall.

A proud father, son, and grandfather, Charles brings his values into every space he steps into. He believes the world of blockchain and cryptocurrency shouldn't be an exclusive club for techies and investors. It should be a wide-open space for parents, teachers, students, small business owners, retirees, dreamers, and doers, anyone ready to learn.

That belief drives Blocks, Coins, and Confidence. This book isn't about flexing technical terms or gatekeeping information. It's a real-world, no-fluff guide to what blockchain is, how coins function, why decentralization matters, and how it is already reshaping our economy, systems, and lives, sometimes in ways we don't even see yet.

⚠ A Note on Investing: Knowledge First

While several chapters of *Blocks, Coins, and Confidence* discuss basic investing concepts, Charles is crystal clear: This book is not financial advice.

The purpose of those chapters is purely educational, to introduce readers to concepts like volatility, wallets, exchanges, and risk management in a rapidly evolving space.

Charles urges readers to always conduct their own research, assess their personal risk tolerance, seek professional guidance when needed, and never invest in anything they do not fully understand. To emphasize this, readers will see this important reminder echoed throughout the book:

"This chapter/book is meant to inform, not to influence your financial decisions. Read with curiosity, move forward cautiously, and always invest wisely."

In a space where reckless promises are all too common, Charles stands firmly in the corner of informed, empowered, and ethical participation.

🌍 A Mission Bigger Than Money

Charles wrote *Blocks, Coins, and Confidence* because he believes education has the power to inform individuals and transform communities and society at large.

He believes that when people truly understand how blockchain and crypto work — when they understand the potential, the risks, and the revolutionary changes already underway — they are better positioned to make responsible choices, innovate boldly, and protect their futures.

He believes real blockchain adoption will not be driven by speculation or hype. It will be driven by understanding, accessibility, and trust, values that can only be built through honest, clear, and fearless education.

"The future of blockchain adoption depends on education. It starts with understanding. That's what this book is all about." — Charles

◐ Guided by Grace. Driven by Purpose.

Above all, Charles lives and works by the words *"Guided by Grace. Driven by Purpose."*

Faith is the foundation for everything he does, but it's never been used to exclude or divide. Instead, it's a quiet, steady force that fuels his humility, compassion, and unwavering commitment to lifting others through knowledge.

Whether leading a classroom discussion, helping a first-time crypto user download a wallet, or collaborating with industry professionals on the future of blockchain education, Charles brings a rare blend of wisdom, warmth, and authenticity to every space he enters.

In a world often filled with noise, he is a voice of calm clarity, passionate, principled, and purpose-driven.

TABLE OF CONTENTS

FOREWORD

As we stand on the brink of a financial revolution, I am both inspired and humbled by the transformative potential of cryptocurrencies and blockchain technology. What was once a niche topic, discussed primarily by tech enthusiasts and libertarians, has now captured the attention of mainstream media, financial institutions, and governments across the globe. The emergence of Bitcoin in 2009 marked the beginning of a new era, challenging traditional notions of money, finance, and the very systems we rely on to transact and store value.

Having spent years as an educator and a passionate advocate for understanding emerging technologies, I felt compelled to write *Blocks, Coins, and Confidence: A Personal Guide to the Crypto Space by an Educator and Enthusiast*. This book is my way of bridging the gap between the complex world of blockchain and cryptocurrency and the everyday individual. Whether you're a complete beginner trying to grasp the fundamentals or an experienced investor looking to sharpen your knowledge, I aim to provide a clear, comprehensive, and practical resource that meets your needs. I'm not covering every aspect of the space, but I'll give you a strong and approachable introduction to crypto and blockchain.

The significance of understanding digital currencies cannot be overstated. As blockchain technology continues to evolve, it's reshaping industries, enhancing transparency, and decentralizing control in ways we couldn't have imagined just a few decades ago. These changes present incredible opportunities, but they also bring challenges that require careful navigation. By understanding these technologies, individuals, businesses, and policymakers can harness their potential while mitigating their risks.

Blocks, Coins, and Confidence was crafted with accessibility and real-world relevance in mind. Inside, you'll find simplified explanations of technical concepts, examples of real-world applications, interviews with industry professionals, and case studies that highlight how blockchain and crypto are being used across different sectors. While this book discusses topics related to investing and innovation, it is intended solely for educational purposes. Readers are encouraged to use the information as a foundation, continue their own research, and consult with trusted professionals when making personal, financial, or business decisions related to cryptocurrency or blockchain technology.

As an educator, I've always believed that learning is about more than just acquiring facts; it's about gaining insights and understanding the broader implications of those facts. This book is as much about the "why" as it is about the "how." Why does blockchain matter? Why are cryptocurrencies reshaping global finance? And how can you, as a learner, investor, or business leader, position yourself to thrive in this new world?

The possibilities that blockchain and digital currencies offer are vast, and they touch virtually every sector—from finance and healthcare to supply chain and education. My hope is that this book inspires you to see the opportunities these technologies provide, while also preparing you to approach them with a critical and informed mindset. This is more than a guide—it's an invitation to become part of a revolution that's reshaping how we think about money, ownership, and trust.

This book represents my dedication to demystifying a field that is often seen as too complex or inaccessible. My aim is to make the concepts understandable, the strategies practical, and the vision for the future tangible. Together, let us embrace the change that cryptocurrencies and blockchain represent, and step boldly into the next era of financial innovation. With knowledge as your foundation, I am confident that you'll understand this new frontier and thrive within it.

INTRODUCTION

The concept of money has undergone significant transformations throughout human history. From bartering goods and services to using precious metals, coins, and paper money, each evolution has aimed to make transactions more efficient and secure. Today, we find ourselves at the brink of another monumental shift: the rise of digital currencies and blockchain technology. This book, "*Blocks, Coins, and Confidence*," is designed to guide you through this exciting new landscape.

Cryptocurrencies, such as Bitcoin and Ethereum, have introduced a decentralized form of money that operates independently of traditional financial institutions. These digital assets leverage blockchain technology to ensure transparency, security, and immutability. As a result, they have the potential to revolutionize not only the financial sector but also various other industries, including supply chain management, healthcare, and voting systems.

Understanding cryptocurrencies and blockchain technology can seem daunting at first. The terminology, technical aspects, and rapid pace of innovation can be overwhelming. However, it is crucial to grasp these concepts as they are increasingly becoming integral to our financial system. This book aims to break down complex ideas into simple, understandable terms, providing you with the knowledge and confidence to navigate the world of digital currency.

Throughout the chapters, we will explore the evolution of money, the fundamentals of blockchain technology, and the intricacies of investing in cryptocurrencies. We will also delve into the practical applications of blockchain beyond digital currencies, examine the regulatory landscape, and look at future trends and innovations. Additionally, you will gain insights from expert interviews and real-world case studies that illustrate the transformative potential of this technology. By the end of this journey, you will be well-equipped to understand and engage with the exciting world of digital currency.

CHAPTER 1

INTRODUCTION:
THE EVOLUTION OF MONEY

Key Points

- Historical Overview
- The Digital Age and Financial Transformation
- Rise of Cryptocurrencies
- Future of Money

CONTENT

Historical Overview

Money has been around for a very long time. In the beginning, people didn't use money like we do today. Instead, they traded things directly. This was called bartering. For example, if you were a farmer with extra vegetables, you might trade them with someone who made shoes. This worked okay, but it was sometimes hard to find someone who wanted what you had and had what you wanted.

As people started trading more, they needed something easier to use. So, they started using things like shells, beads, and eventually metals like gold and silver. These were better because everyone agreed they were valuable, and they were easier to carry around. People began making coins out of these metals, and each coin had a specific value. This made trading much simpler and more organized.

Eventually, carrying a lot of coins became a problem, especially if you were trading large amounts. So, people started using paper money. The first known paper money was used in China over a thousand years ago. Paper money was much lighter and easier to carry than coins. Each piece of paper money represented a certain amount of gold or silver stored somewhere safe.

Paper money quickly spread around the world. Governments and banks started printing their own paper money, and it became the standard way to pay for things. This made trade and commerce much easier and helped economies grow. Over time, people got used to using paper money, and it became an essential part of everyday life.

As economies grew and technology advanced, new forms of money and financial systems were developed. This led to the creation of digital forms of money and the transformation of the financial industry, setting the stage for the next major evolution in money: the digital age.

The Digital Age and Financial Transformation

With the invention of computers and the internet, money started changing again. Banks began using computers to keep track of people's money. This made managing money much easier and faster. People could now transfer money electronically without having to carry cash. This was the beginning of electronic banking.

Then came credit cards and debit cards. These cards made it even easier to spend money. Credit cards let you borrow money from the bank up to a certain limit, which you would pay back later. Debit cards allow you to spend money directly from your bank account. Both types of cards made buying things quicker and safer than using cash.

As technology continued to advance, online banking became popular. People could now manage their bank accounts from their computers at home. This meant they could check their balances, pay bills, and transfer money without going to the bank. Mobile banking apps on smartphones made it even more convenient, allowing people to do all these things from anywhere.

The rise of the internet also brought about new ways to shop and do business. Online stores and e-commerce platforms became popular, allowing people to buy and sell goods and services from the comfort of their homes. This digital transformation made the economy more interconnected and global, with money moving quickly across borders.

Digital payments and electronic transfers became the norm. People could send and receive money instantly using online services like PayPal and mobile payment apps. This made financial transactions faster and opened up new opportunities for businesses and consumers, making the financial system more efficient and accessible.

The Rise of Cryptocurrencies

In 2009, a new kind of money was invented called Bitcoin.

Bitcoin is a type of **cryptocurrency**, which means it's a digital form of money that exists only online. What makes it different from the dollars in your wallet or the balance in your bank account is that it was built to be **decentralized**, meaning no single person, company, or government has control over it.

Bitcoin was created by someone using the name **Satoshi Nakamoto**, a mysterious figure (or possibly a group) whose identity remains unknown to this day. But one thing is clear: Satoshi didn't just create a new type of money; he introduced a new mindset around **trust, independence, and control over our finances**.

Instead of relying on banks or governments, Bitcoin runs on a public technology called **blockchain**. Think of blockchain as a giant *digital ledger* (or notebook, to make it simple) open for everyone to see. This notebook (*digital ledger*) records every single transaction ever made with Bitcoin. The pages of this notebook (*digital ledger*) are called "**blocks**," and they're linked together to form a chain, hence the name, *blockchain*. Once something's written in the book (*digital ledger*), it can't be erased or changed. That makes it incredibly **secure** and **transparent**.

Because of this setup, cheating the system is almost impossible. You can't fake a transaction, steal coins without being noticed, or secretly rewrite history. And the best part? It doesn't matter where in the world you are, **Bitcoin works globally**. You don't need a bank. You just need internet access and a digital wallet.

📄 The White Paper That Changed Everything

Before Bitcoin launched, Satoshi Nakamoto published the Bitcoin White Paper in 2008. It was titled Bitcoin: A Peer-to-Peer Electronic Cash System and laid out the entire vision for this new digital currency.

You can read it yourself at bitcoin.org/bitcoin.pdf.

Since Bitcoin's launch, **thousands of other cryptocurrencies** have been created. Some are designed to process payments faster, others focus on privacy, and a few power entire ecosystems of apps and smart contracts. Each one has its own unique features and purpose.

Cryptocurrencies can now be used to:

- Buy things online (and sometimes in stores)
- Send money to people anywhere in the world, quickly and with low fees
- Invest and build wealth (though prices can go way up and down)
- Build and use decentralized apps that don't rely on big tech companies or banks

They offer a lot of advantages over traditional money. For starters, they're not tied to any single country or bank. That makes them especially useful in places where the local currency is unstable, or where people don't have access to bank accounts. And because crypto operates on the internet, **it works everywhere**, it's fast, borderless, and open to everyone.

But let's be real for a second: crypto **can also be confusing**. There's a lot to learn. Prices can swing wildly. And not every project is worth your time or money. That's why **education matters so much in this space**—and why this book exists.

We're witnessing the rise of a bold, new world.

One where people are rethinking how money should work.

One where financial power isn't locked away behind a bank teller's glass or restricted by borders.

One where everyday people are invited to the table.

As more people started using and investing in cryptocurrencies, their value rose. That rise caught the attention of investors, big businesses, and even governments. Today, cryptocurrencies are no longer a fringe idea, they're a **major part of the global financial system**, and their influence is only growing.

And this is just the beginning.

Future of Money

The future of money is very exciting and full of possibilities. Cryptocurrencies and blockchain technology might change how we think about and use money. For example, digital wallets on our smartphones could become the main way we manage our money. These wallets can store different types of cryptocurrencies and make it easy to pay for things with a simple tap.

Another exciting development is decentralized finance, or DeFi. DeFi uses blockchain technology to create financial services like lending and borrowing without needing traditional banks. This could make financial services more accessible to people all over the world, especially those who don't have access to banks.

As more people and businesses start using cryptocurrencies, governments are also looking into creating their own digital currencies. These central bank digital currencies (CBDCs) would combine the benefits of cryptocurrencies with the stability of traditional money. The way we use and think about money will continue to evolve, and the future holds many exciting possibilities.

There are also other technological advancements on the horizon, such as artificial intelligence (AI) and the Internet of Things (IoT), that could further change how we use money. AI could help us make better financial decisions, while IoT devices could automate payments and transactions, making our lives even more convenient.

The future of money will likely be a mix of traditional and digital forms. As we continue to embrace new technologies, we must also address challenges such as security, privacy, and regulation. By doing so, we can create a financial system that is more inclusive, efficient, and secure for everyone.

SUMMARY OF CHAPTER 1

Money has changed a lot over time. It started with bartering, where people traded items like fruits for shoes. Then, people began using things like shells, beads, and metals like gold and silver as money because they were easier to carry and everyone agreed they were valuable. Coins made trading simpler, and later, paper money, which was lighter, made buying and selling even easier.

With computers and the internet, money has changed again. Banks used computers to manage money, and people could transfer money electronically. Credit cards and debit cards have made spending money safer and more convenient. Online banking allows people to manage their money from computers and smartphones.

In 2009, Bitcoin was created as a new type of money that exists only online, called a cryptocurrency. It uses blockchain technology to keep transactions secure. Since then, many other cryptocurrencies have been developed, allowing people to buy things, invest, and send money quickly and cheaply.

The future of money is exciting. We might use digital wallets on our phones to manage different types of digital money. New technologies like decentralized finance (DeFi) could allow people to borrow and lend money without banks. Governments are also considering creating their own digital currencies. In short, money has evolved from bartering to digital transactions, and cryptocurrencies are the latest development, offering new ways to use and think about money. The future looks promising with many new possibilities.

CHAPTER 1'S QUOTE:

"Bitcoin is a technological tour de force."

– Bill Gates

CHAPTER 1'S DEFINITIONS TO REMEMBER:

1. Bartering: Exchanging goods and services directly without using money.
2. Cryptocurrency: A digital currency that uses cryptography for security and operates independently of a central bank.
3. Blockchain: A digital ledger where transactions are recorded chronologically and publicly.
4. Electronic Banking: Managing bank accounts and transactions using computers and the internet.
5. Digital Wallet: An app or device that stores payment information and allows for digital transactions.
6. Decentralized Finance (DeFi): Financial services that operate without a central authority, using blockchain technology.

QUIZ: CHAPTER 1

Introduction: The Evolution of Money

1. **What was one of the first forms of money used in human history?**

   a) Credit cards

   b) Bartering, where people exchanged goods and services directly

   c) Paper money

   d) Digital wallets

2. **How did the digital age change the way we use money?**

   a) It made bartering more common

   b) The digital age introduced electronic banking, credit and debit cards, and mobile payments, making transactions more convenient and secure

   c) People stopped using money altogether

   d) Only governments could use digital money

3. **What makes cryptocurrencies different from traditional money?**

   a) Cryptocurrencies are physical coins issued by banks

   b) Cryptocurrencies are digital, decentralized, and use blockchain technology, making them independent of governments and banks

   c) Cryptocurrencies are only used for bartering

   d) Cryptocurrencies are the same as credit cards

4. **What are some possible future developments in the way we use money?**

   a) A return to bartering and gold coins

   b) Wider adoption of digital wallets, growth of decentralized finance (DeFi), and the introduction of central bank digital currencies (CBDCs)

   c) Only using cash for all transactions

   d) Eliminating all forms of digital payments

5. **What is the technology behind cryptocurrencies?**

   a) Paper ledgers

   b) Blockchain, a secure and transparent digital ledger

   c) Magnetic strips on cards

   d) Physical vaults

6. **How do digital wallets enhance the way we manage our finances?**

   a) By storing only cash

   b) By securely storing multiple forms of currency and offering features like budgeting tools and biometric authentication

   c) By limiting spending options

   d) By making transactions slower

7. **What are the potential benefits and challenges of decentralized finance (DeFi)?**

   a) Benefits include lower fees and greater transparency; challenges include regulatory uncertainty and security risks

   b) Only benefits, no challenges

   c) Only challenges, no benefits

   d) DeFi is unrelated to finance

8. **Who created Bitcoin, and why is their identity still a mystery?**

    a) Elon Musk, for social media experiments

    b) Satoshi Nakamoto, a pseudonymous creator who wanted to build decentralized money outside traditional banking

    c) The U.S. Federal Reserve, to track online payments

    d) Jeff Bezos, to launch Amazon Pay

9. **What was the original purpose behind Bitcoin's creation?**

    a) To help governments collect taxes faster

    b) To allow banks to charge higher transaction fees

    c) To create a peer-to-peer financial system that doesn't rely on centralized banks or intermediaries

    d) To replace gold with a digital currency backed by oil

10. **What is blockchain, and why is it important?**

    a) A private server used by big tech companies

    b) A video game platform that rewards users with tokens

    c) A secure, public digital ledger that records every cryptocurrency transaction in a tamper-proof way

    d) A new kind of search engine for cryptocurrency websites

11. **What makes blockchain secure and transparent?**

    a) Each transaction is verified by a single bank officer

    b) Everyone can view the blockchain, but no one can change past records

    c) Transactions are hidden from the public

    d) It's protected by armed guards and password folders

12. **Why can't someone easily cheat the Bitcoin system?**

    a) Because Bitcoin is backed by a global insurance policy

    b) Because there are human moderators checking each payment

    c) Because blockchain makes it nearly impossible to alter transaction records without detection

    d) Because every Bitcoin transaction must be mailed in and notarized

13. **What is the Bitcoin White Paper and where can it be found?**

    a) A historical timeline of paper currencies—available at the Library of Congress

    b) A comic book about Bitcoin published by Marvel

    c) A document written by Satoshi Nakamoto that explains how Bitcoin works—available at bitcoin.org/bitcoin.pdf

    d) A confidential document used only by banks

14. **Why are cryptocurrencies especially helpful in regions with limited access to banking?**

    a) Because they are physical coins mailed to remote areas

    b) Because they can only be used by governments

    c) Because they don't require traditional bank accounts and can be accessed from anywhere with the internet

    d) Because they are printed in multiple languages

☑ ANSWER KEY WITH DETAILED EXPLANATIONS

1. b) Bartering, where people exchanged goods and services directly

    Explanation:

    Before money, people traded goods and services directly, known as bartering, which was the earliest form of exchange.

2. b) The digital age introduced electronic banking, credit and debit cards, and mobile payments, making transactions more convenient and secure

    Explanation:

    Technology transformed money management, enabling electronic banking and digital payments that are faster and safer than cash.

3. b) Cryptocurrencies are digital, decentralized, and use blockchain technology, making them independent of governments and banks

    Explanation:

    Unlike traditional money, cryptocurrencies operate on decentralized networks and use blockchain for secure, transparent transactions.

4. b) Wider adoption of digital wallets, growth of decentralized finance (DeFi), and the introduction of central bank digital currencies (CBDCs)

    Explanation:

    The future of money includes digital wallets, blockchain-based financial services, and government-issued digital currencies.

5. **b) Blockchain, a secure and transparent digital ledger**
    Explanation:
    Blockchain is the underlying technology for cryptocurrencies, providing a secure and public record of all transactions.

6. **b) By securely storing multiple forms of currency and offering features like budgeting tools and biometric authentication**
    Explanation:
    Digital wallets help users manage various currencies and provide extra features for convenience and security.

7. **a) Benefits include lower fees and greater transparency; challenges include regulatory uncertainty and security risks**
    Explanation:
    DeFi offers cost savings and transparency but faces issues like unclear regulations and the need for robust security.

8. **b) Satoshi Nakamoto, a pseudonymous creator who wanted to build decentralized money outside traditional banking**
    Explanation:
    Bitcoin was introduced by someone using the name Satoshi Nakamoto, a mysterious figure (or group) whose identity is still unknown. Satoshi didn't just create a new type of money—he introduced a new mindset around trust, independence, and control over our finances.

9. **c) To create a peer-to-peer financial system that doesn't rely on centralized banks or intermediaries**
    Explanation:
    Bitcoin was created in response to the 2008 financial crisis. The goal was to create peer-to-peer digital cash that could be sent directly from one person to another without banks, credit card companies, or middlemen.

10. c) **A secure, public digital ledger that records every cryptocurrency transaction in a tamper-proof way**

    Explanation:

    Blockchain is a public system that records every transaction. Think of it like a giant digital notebook that's open for everyone to see. Once something's written in the book, it can't be erased or changed. That makes it incredibly secure and transparent.

11. b) **Everyone can view the blockchain, but no one can change past records**

    Explanation:

    Blockchain's structure ensures that everyone can see the records, but no one can alter them. This makes it very hard to cheat or steal Bitcoin and builds trust in the system.

12. c) **Because blockchain makes it nearly impossible to alter transaction records without detection**

    Explanation:

    You can't fake a transaction, steal coins without being noticed, or secretly rewrite history. Blockchain technology makes cheating the system nearly impossible.

13. c) **A document written by Satoshi Nakamoto that explains how Bitcoin works—available at bitcoin.org/bitcoin.pdf**

    Explanation:

    Before Bitcoin ever launched, Satoshi Nakamoto published a document called the Bitcoin White Paper. It's titled *Bitcoin: A Peer-to-Peer Electronic Cash System* and can be read at bitcoin.org/bitcoin.pdf.

14. c) **Because they don't require traditional bank accounts and can be accessed from anywhere with the internet**

Explanation:

Cryptocurrencies are especially helpful for people who don't have access to banks or who live in countries with unstable currencies. They're global, borderless, and open to anyone with internet access.

CHAPTER 2

UNDERSTANDING CRYPTOCURRENCY

Key Points

- What is Cryptocurrency?
- Key Cryptocurrencies: Bitcoin, Ethereum, and Beyond
- How Cryptocurrencies Work
- Benefits and Drawbacks

CONTENT

What is Cryptocurrency?

Cryptocurrency is a type of digital or virtual money that uses special technology called cryptography to keep transactions secure and to control the creation of new units. Unlike traditional money, which is issued by governments and banks, cryptocurrencies operate on a technology called blockchain, which is decentralized. This means that no single person, company, or government controls them.

Cryptocurrencies exist only in digital form. This means you can't hold a physical coin or bill. Instead, you use a digital wallet to store, send, and receive these digital coins. Each cryptocurrency transaction is recorded on a public ledger called a blockchain. This ledger is maintained by a network of computers around the world, making it very secure and transparent.

One of the key features of cryptocurrencies is that they are decentralized. Traditional currencies, like the US dollar or the Euro, are controlled by central banks and governments. They can print more money and regulate its value. Cryptocurrencies, on the other hand, are created through a process called mining, where powerful computers solve complex problems to add new transactions to the blockchain. This makes cryptocurrencies more resistant to control or interference.

Another important aspect of cryptocurrencies is that they use cryptography to secure transactions. Cryptography is a method of protecting information by transforming it into a code. This ensures that all transactions are secure and that only the intended recipient can access the funds. This high level of security is one reason why cryptocurrencies have become popular.

Cryptocurrencies can be used for many purposes. People use them to buy goods and services, invest in projects, or send money to friends and family quickly and cheaply. Some people like cryptocurrencies because they offer more privacy than traditional financial systems. Others see them as a way to make money by investing in new and growing technologies.

Key Cryptocurrencies: Bitcoin, Ethereum, and Beyond

Bitcoin was the first cryptocurrency and is still the most well-known and widely used. It was created in 2009 by an unknown person or group using the name Satoshi Nakamoto. Bitcoin was designed to be a digital version of cash that could be sent from person to person without needing a bank or other intermediary. Bitcoin transactions are verified by network nodes through cryptography and recorded on the blockchain.

Ethereum is another popular cryptocurrency created by Vitalik Buterin in 2015. Ethereum is different from Bitcoin because it is a digital currency and a platform for creating decentralized applications (dApps). These applications run on the Ethereum blockchain and can perform various tasks without needing a central authority. The currency used on the Ethereum platform is called Ether (ETH).

There are thousands of other cryptocurrencies, each with its unique features and uses. For example, Ripple (XRP) is designed for fast and low-cost international money transfers. Litecoin (LTC) was created to be the "silver to Bitcoin's gold" and offers faster transaction times. Cardano (ADA) aims to provide a more secure and scalable platform for developing decentralized applications and smart contracts.

Some cryptocurrencies are focused on privacy. For example, Monero (XMR) and Zcash (ZEC) offer enhanced privacy features that make it difficult to trace transactions. Others, like Binance Coin (BNB), are used to pay for cryptocurrency exchange transactions and offer users discounts.

Each cryptocurrency has its strengths and weaknesses, and people choose which ones to use or invest in based on their needs and preferences. The diversity of cryptocurrencies means a wide range of options are available for different purposes.

How Cryptocurrencies Work

Cryptocurrencies operate on a technology called blockchain. A blockchain is a digital ledger that records all transactions across a network of computers. Each transaction is added to a block, and once the block is full, it is added to the chain of previous blocks. This creates a continuous and secure record of all transactions.

When you send cryptocurrency to someone, the transaction is broadcast to the entire network. Miners, who are network participants with powerful computers, verify the transaction by solving complex mathematical problems. Once the transaction is verified, it is added to a block and then to the blockchain. This process is known as mining, and it ensures that all transactions are secure and cannot be changed or deleted.

Cryptocurrencies use a pair of cryptographic keys: a public key and a private key. The public key is like an address that you can share with others to receive cryptocurrency. The private key is a secret code that you use to sign transactions and access your funds. It is important to keep your private key secure because anyone who has it can control your cryptocurrency.

Digital wallets are used to store, send, and receive cryptocurrencies. There are different types of wallets, including software wallets (apps on your phone or computer), hardware wallets (physical devices), and paper wallets (printed QR codes). Each type has its security features and trade-offs, but all wallets help you manage your cryptocurrencies safely.

One of the advantages of cryptocurrencies is that they allow for peer-to-peer transactions without needing a bank or other intermediary. This can make transactions faster and cheaper, especially for international transfers. However, because cryptocurrencies are still new and their value can change rapidly, they can also be risky.

Benefits and Drawbacks

Cryptocurrencies offer several benefits. One of the main advantages is that they are decentralized and not controlled by any government or bank. This means they can be more resistant to censorship and interference. Transactions can be made quickly and cheaply, especially for international transfers. Cryptocurrencies also offer more privacy than traditional financial systems, as transactions do not require personal information.

Another benefit is the potential for high returns on investment. Many people have made significant profits by investing in cryptocurrencies, especially those who bought Bitcoin or Ethereum early on. Cryptocurrencies can also be utilized to develop new types of financial services and applications, thereby opening up opportunities for innovation and entrepreneurship.

However, there are also drawbacks to cryptocurrencies. One of the main challenges is their volatility. The value of cryptocurrencies can change rapidly, making them risky investments. This volatility can be caused by various factors, including market speculation, regulatory changes, and technological developments.

Security is another concern. While blockchain technology is very secure, individual users must take precautions to protect their private keys and wallets. There have been cases of hacks and scams where people have lost their cryptocurrencies. Additionally, because transactions are irreversible, mistakes cannot be easily corrected.

Regulation is also an issue. Cryptocurrencies operate in a legal gray area in many countries, and governments are still figuring out how to regulate them. This uncertainty can create risks for users and investors. There is also the potential for illegal activities, such as money laundering and tax evasion, which governments are keen to prevent.

SUMMARY

Cryptocurrencies are a new form of digital money that uses cryptography and blockchain technology to operate securely and independently of traditional financial systems. Bitcoin and Ethereum are two of the most popular cryptocurrencies, each with unique features and uses. Bitcoin was designed as a decentralized digital currency, while Ethereum supports smart contracts and decentralized applications (dApps).

Cryptocurrencies offer several benefits, including decentralization, enhanced privacy, and the potential for high returns on investment. They enable fast and inexpensive transactions without the need for intermediaries like banks, especially for international transfers. However, they also come with risks such as price volatility, security concerns, and regulatory uncertainty.

Understanding how cryptocurrencies work—through blockchain technology, mining processes, and cryptographic keys—along with their benefits and drawbacks can help you navigate this exciting new world of digital finance.

QUOTE

"Bitcoin is the beginning of something great: a currency without a government, something necessary and imperative."

– Nassim Nicholas Taleb

DEFINITIONS

1. Cryptography: Securing information by converting it into a coded format that can only be read by someone with the key to decode it.

2. Mining: The process by which transactions are verified and added to the public ledger (blockchain) and new cryptocurrency units are generated.

3. Public Key: A publicly accessible key that allows others to send you cryptocurrency.

4. Private Key: A secret key that allows you to access and manage your cryptocurrency.

5. Node: A computer participating in the blockchain network, validating and relaying transactions.

6. Smart Contract: Self-executing contracts with the terms directly written into code, running on a blockchain.

QUIZ: CHAPTER 2

Understanding Cryptocurrency

1. **What is cryptocurrency, and how does it differ from traditional money?**

   a) Cryptocurrency is physical money issued by governments.

   b) Cryptocurrency is a digital or virtual form of money that uses cryptography for security and operates on a decentralized network, unlike traditional money, which is issued and controlled by governments and central banks.

   c) Cryptocurrency is only used for online gaming.

   d) Cryptocurrency is a type of credit card.

2. **What are the key features of Bitcoin and Ethereum?**

   a) Bitcoin is a government-backed digital currency, and Ethereum is used only for online shopping.

   b) Bitcoin is a decentralized digital currency designed as a store of value and medium of exchange, while Ethereum is a decentralized platform that supports smart contracts and decentralized applications (dApps).

   c) Both are physical coins you can hold.

   d) Bitcoin and Ethereum are both used only for anonymous transactions.

3. **How does blockchain technology ensure the security and transparency of cryptocurrency transactions?**

   a) By keeping all transactions secret and unrecorded.

   b) By using a distributed ledger that is resistant to tampering and ensures that the network verifies all transactions, making records secure and transparent.

   c) By allowing only one company to control all records.

   d) By deleting transaction records after one year.

4. **What are the benefits of using cryptocurrencies for transactions?**

   a) Decentralization, security, accessibility, fast and low-cost transactions, and the potential for innovation through smart contracts and dApps.

   b) Guaranteed profits and government insurance.

   c) Unlimited refunds and reversals.

   d) Only usable within one country.

5. **What are some of the drawbacks and challenges associated with cryptocurrencies?**

   a) No risks or challenges.

   b) Price volatility, regulatory uncertainty, security risks, high energy consumption, and scalability issues.

   c) Guaranteed value increase.

   d) No need for secure storage.

☑ ANSWER KEY WITH DETAILED EXPLANATIONS

1. b) Cryptocurrency is a digital or virtual form of money that uses cryptography for security and operates on a decentralized network, unlike traditional money, which is issued and controlled by governments and central banks.

    Explanation:

    Cryptocurrencies are digital, secured by cryptography, and decentralized, making them fundamentally different from government-issued physical money.

2. b) Bitcoin is a decentralized digital currency designed as a store of value and medium of exchange, while Ethereum is a decentralized platform that supports smart contracts and decentralized applications (dApps).

    Explanation:

    Bitcoin's primary use is as a digital currency, while Ethereum offers a platform for building decentralized applications in addition to its own currency, Ether.

3. b) By using a distributed ledger that is resistant to tampering and ensures that the network verifies all transactions, making records secure and transparent.

    Explanation:

    Blockchain technology secures transactions by distributing records across a network, making them transparent and hard to alter.

4. a) **Decentralization, security, accessibility, fast and low-cost transactions, and the potential for innovation through smart contracts and dApps.**

    Explanation:

    Cryptocurrencies offer several benefits, including speed, lower costs, global access, and new possibilities for financial innovation.

5. b) **Price volatility, regulatory uncertainty, security risks, high energy consumption, and scalability issues.**

    Explanation:

    Cryptocurrencies face significant challenges such as rapid price changes, unclear regulations, security threats, energy use, and technical limitations.

CHAPTER 3

BLOCKCHAIN TECHNOLOGY EXPLAINED

Key Points

- The Fundamentals of Blockchain
- Blockchain vs. Traditional Databases
- Applications Beyond Cryptocurrency
- Future of Blockchain Technology

The Fundamentals of Blockchain

Blockchain technology is the backbone of cryptocurrencies, but its uses go far beyond digital money. A blockchain is a type of digital ledger that records transactions across many computers. These transactions are grouped together in blocks, and each block is linked to the one before it, forming a chain of blocks. This is why it is called a blockchain.

One of a blockchain's most important features is its decentralization. This means that no single person, company, or government controls it. Instead, all the computers in the network work together to verify and record transactions. This makes blockchain very secure because it is difficult for anyone to alter the records without being noticed by the entire network.

Another key feature of blockchain is that it is transparent. Anyone can view the transactions recorded on a public blockchain. This transparency helps to build trust because it is easy to see that the records are accurate and have not been tampered with. However, the identities of the people making the transactions can remain private.n

The process of adding new transactions to the blockchain is called mining. Miners use powerful computers to solve complex mathematical problems. When they solve these problems, they add a new block of transactions to the blockchain and are rewarded with new cryptocurrency. This process ensures that all transactions are verified and secure.

Blockchain technology also uses cryptographic hashing, a method of turning information into a unique string of characters. This ensures that each block of transactions is secure and cannot be changed. If someone tries to alter a transaction, the hash will change, and the entire network will know that something is wrong.

Blockchain vs. Traditional Databases

Blockchain technology is different from traditional databases in several important ways. A traditional database is usually controlled by a single entity, such as a company or a government. This central control can make the database vulnerable to hacking, fraud, or other types of tampering.

In contrast, a blockchain is decentralized. This means that no single entity has control over the entire network. Instead, many computers work together to verify and record transactions. This makes blockchain much more secure because it is very difficult for anyone to alter the records without being noticed by the entire network.

Another difference is how data is stored and verified. In a traditional database, data is stored in a central location and can be changed or deleted by authorized users. In a blockchain, data is stored in blocks that are linked together in a chain. Once a block is added to the blockchain, it cannot be changed or deleted. This makes blockchain records permanent and tamper-proof.

Blockchain also provides greater transparency. In a traditional database, users must trust the central authority to keep accurate and honest records. In a blockchain, anyone can view the transactions recorded on the public ledger. This transparency helps to build trust because it is easy to see that the records are accurate and have not been tampered with.

However, blockchain technology has some drawbacks compared to traditional databases. It can be slower and less efficient because many computers must verify all transactions. This can also make it more expensive to operate. Additionally, because blockchain is still a relatively new technology, it can be more complicated to use and understand.

Applications Beyond Cryptocurrency

While blockchain technology was first developed for cryptocurrencies like Bitcoin, its uses go far beyond digital money. One of the most promising applications of blockchain is in supply chain management. By using blockchain, companies can track products from the manufacturer to the consumer, ensuring that they are authentic and have not been tampered with.

Another important application of blockchain is in healthcare. Blockchain can be used to securely store and share patient records, making it easier for doctors and hospitals to access important information. This can improve the quality of care and reduce the risk of errors.

Voting systems are another area where blockchain can be useful. By using blockchain, governments can create secure and transparent voting systems that are resistant to fraud. This can help to ensure that elections are fair and accurate.

Blockchain can also be used to create smart contracts. These are contracts that automatically execute when certain conditions are met. For example, a smart contract could be used to automatically release payment when a product is delivered. This can reduce the need for intermediaries and make transactions faster and more efficient.

Future of Blockchain Technology

The future of blockchain technology is very exciting. As more people and companies learn about blockchain and its potential, we can expect to see many new and innovative uses for this technology. One area of development is scalability. Currently, blockchain networks can be slow and expensive to operate, but researchers are working on ways to make them faster and more efficient.

Another area of development is interoperability. This means making it easier for different blockchain networks to work together. By improving interoperability, we can create a more connected and efficient blockchain ecosystem.

Security will also continue to be a major focus. While blockchain is already very secure, researchers are always looking for ways to make it even more secure. This includes developing new cryptographic methods and improving how blockchain networks verify transactions.

Finally, we can expect to see more regulation and oversight of blockchain technology. As blockchain becomes more widely used, governments and regulatory bodies must develop new rules and guidelines to ensure that it is used safely and responsibly.

In conclusion, blockchain technology is a revolutionary innovation that has the potential to transform many different industries. By understanding how blockchain works and its many applications, we can better appreciate its potential and prepare for the exciting changes that lie ahead.

SUMMARY

Blockchain technology is a secure way to record transactions and data. Unlike traditional databases, it is decentralized and transparent, enhancing security and trust. Transactions are grouped into blocks linked together in a chain, making the records tamper-proof.

Key features of blockchain include decentralization, cryptographic hashing, and transparency. Decentralization ensures that no single entity controls the network. Cryptographic hashing secures the data, and transparency allows public verification of transactions.

Beyond cryptocurrency, blockchain can be used in supply chain management, healthcare, and voting systems, providing secure and efficient ways to track and verify information.

The future of blockchain looks promising. Improvements in scalability, interoperability, and security will make it a transformative technology for various industries. Understanding blockchain's fundamentals and applications highlights its potential impact on the future.

QUOTE

"The blockchain does one thing: It replaces third-party trust with mathematical proof that something happened."

– Adam Draper

DEFINITIONS

1. **Decentralized**: A system that operates without a central authority, spreading control across multiple participants or nodes. This is a key feature of blockchain technology, making it more secure and resistant to tampering.

2. **Cryptographic Hashing**: A process that converts data into a fixed-size string of characters, which is unique to the input data. It is used in blockchain to secure transactions and link blocks in the chain.

3. **Consensus Mechanism**: A protocol that ensures all nodes in a blockchain network agree on the validity of transactions. Examples include Proof of Work (PoW) and Proof of Stake (PoS).

4. **Ledger**: A record-keeping system that maintains a continuously growing list of transactions or records. In blockchain, the ledger is distributed and decentralized, ensuring transparency and security.

5. **Interoperability**: The ability of different blockchain networks to work together and exchange information. This is important for creating a more connected and efficient blockchain ecosystem.

6. **Scalability**: The capacity of a blockchain network to handle a growing amount of transactions efficiently. Improving scalability is a major focus in blockchain development to support wider adoption.

7. **Transparency**: The characteristic of being open and accessible for anyone to verify the transactions or data recorded. Blockchain's transparency helps build trust as all transactions are publicly recorded.

QUIZ: CHAPTER 3

Blockchain Technology Explained

1. What is blockchain technology, and how is it different from traditional databases?

    a) Blockchain is a centralized database managed by a single authority.

    b) Blockchain is a decentralized digital ledger that records transactions across many computers, making it more secure and transparent than traditional databases, which are usually controlled by a single entity.

    c) Blockchain is only used for storing cryptocurrency prices.

    d) Blockchain allows anyone to delete or change records at any time.

2. What makes blockchain secure and tamper-proof?

    a) All transactions are kept secret and hidden from the public.

    b) Blockchain uses cryptographic hashing and a decentralized network of computers to verify and record transactions, making it very difficult to alter the records without being noticed by the entire network.

    c) Only one company controls the blockchain.

    d) Blockchain records are stored on a single server.

3. **Which of the following are applications of blockchain technology beyond cryptocurrency?**

   a) Only for trading digital coins

   b) Supply chain management, healthcare, voting systems, and smart contracts

   c) Sending emails

   d) Managing personal calendars

4. **What are some of the future developments expected in blockchain technology?**

   a) Decreasing security and transparency

   b) Improvements in scalability, interoperability, security, and regulation

   c) Eliminating decentralization

   d) Making blockchain records easier to tamper with

5. **How does a smart contract work?**

   a) It requires a lawyer to manually approve every transaction.

   b) It is a self-executing contract with the terms directly written into code. It automatically executes when certain conditions are met, reducing the need for intermediaries.

   c) It is a paper contract stored in a database.

   d) It only applies to cryptocurrency mining.

☑ ANSWER KEY WITH DETAILED EXPLANATIONS

1. b) Blockchain is a decentralized digital ledger that records transactions across many computers, making it more secure and transparent than traditional databases, which are usually controlled by a single entity.

   Explanation:

   Blockchain's decentralization and transparency set it apart from traditional, centrally controlled databases.

2. b) Blockchain uses cryptographic hashing and a decentralized network of computers to verify and record transactions, making it very difficult to alter the records without being noticed by the entire network.

   Explanation:

   Security comes from cryptographic hashing and decentralization, making tampering extremely difficult.

3. b) Supply chain management, healthcare, voting systems, and smart contracts

   Explanation:

   Blockchain has applications far beyond cryptocurrency, including tracking products, securing health records, enabling transparent voting, and automating contracts.

4. b) Improvements in scalability, interoperability, security, and regulation

   Explanation:

   The future of blockchain includes making networks faster, more connected, more secure, and appropriately regulated.

5. b) It is a self-executing contract with the terms directly written into code. It automatically executes when certain conditions are met, reducing the need for intermediaries.

    Explanation:

    Smart contracts automate transactions based on coded rules, increasing efficiency and reducing the need for third parties

CHAPTER 4

INVESTING IN CRYPTOCURRENCY

Key Points

- Investment Strategies
- Risks and Rewards
- Building a Crypto Portfolio
- Diversification Tips

CONTENT

Investment Strategies

Investing in cryptocurrency can be exciting and profitable, but it's essential to have a strategy. One popular strategy is **buying and holding**. This means purchasing cryptocurrency and keeping it for a long time, hoping its value will increase. This strategy is often used with well-known cryptocurrencies like Bitcoin and Ethereum. The idea is to hold through market ups and downs, banking on long-term growth.

Another strategy is **trading**, which involves buying and selling cryptocurrencies over short periods to take advantage of price fluctuations. Traders use technical analysis, studying charts and patterns, to predict price movements. This strategy requires more time and knowledge than buying and holding. Successful trading also involves understanding market trends, news, and investor sentiment, which can be volatile and unpredictable.

Dollar-cost averaging (DCA) is a strategy where you invest a fixed amount of money in cryptocurrency at regular intervals, regardless of the price. This approach reduces the impact of market volatility and avoids the risk of investing a large amount at the wrong time. By spreading out your investments, you can potentially lower your average purchase price over time, mitigating some risks of sudden market drops.

Staking is another strategy where you hold certain cryptocurrencies in a wallet to support the network's operations, like validating transactions. In return, you earn rewards, similar to earning interest on a savings account. Staking can provide a steady stream of income, but it's essential to understand the specific requirements and risks associated with the cryptocurrency you're staking.

A popular term in the crypto community is **HODL**, which stands for "Hold On for Dear Life." Originally a typo from a Bitcoin forum post in 2013, it has come to mean holding onto your cryptocurrency investment despite market volatility. HODLing is a long-term investment strategy that involves keeping your cryptocurrency through ups and downs, with the belief that the value will increase significantly over time.

An important rule in crypto investing is to **only invest what you can afford to lose**. Cryptocurrencies are highly volatile and speculative. Never invest money that you need for essential expenses or cannot afford to lose. Be conservative until you understand and are comfortable with crypto invest-ing. Start small, learn, and then consider increasing your investment as you gain confidence and knowledge.

> **Important Disclaimer:** *The information provided in this section is for educational and informational purposes only and should not be con-strued as financial or investment advice. Always conduct your own re-search and consult with a licensed financial advisor before making in-vestment decisions.*

Risks and Rewards

Investing in cryptocurrency offers high potential rewards but also comes with significant risks. One of the main rewards is the potential for substan-tial returns. Cryptocurrencies like Bitcoin have seen massive price increases, making early investors very wealthy. These gains attract many new investors looking to replicate that success.

However, the risks are also considerable. **Volatility** is one of the biggest risks. Cryptocurrency prices can fluctuate wildly in short periods, leading to significant losses. This volatility can be due to market speculation, regula-tory news, technological advancements, or macroeconomic trends. Under-standing these factors can help manage the inherent risks.

Security risks are another concern. While blockchain technology is secure, individual users must protect their wallets and private keys to avoid hacks and thefts. Many investors have lost their assets due to phishing scams, mal-ware, and other security breaches. Using hardware wallets and following best security practices can mitigate these risks.

Regulatory uncertainty is also a risk. Governments around the world are still figuring out how to regulate cryptocurrencies, and new regulations could impact their value and use. Regulatory news can cause market volatility as investors react to potential changes in the legal environment. Staying informed about regulatory developments is crucial for managing this risk.

Market manipulation is another risk, where prices are artificially inflated or deflated by large investors, often referred to as "whales." These manipulations can lead to significant price swings, creating opportunities and risks for retail investors. Awareness of market dynamics and careful analysis can help navigate these challenges.

Additionally, cryptocurrencies face **technological risks**. Bugs, network attacks, and technological changes can impact the functionality and security of a cryptocurrency. Investing in well-established projects with strong security measures can reduce these risks.

Lastly, the risk of **missing out** (FOMO) can lead to poor investment decisions. The fear of missing out on potential gains can drive investors to buy at high prices or sell at low prices, leading to losses. Developing a disciplined investment strategy and sticking to it can help avoid impulsive decisions driven by market emotions.

Building a Crypto Portfolio

Building a diversified crypto portfolio can help manage risks. A good portfolio might include a mix of established cryptocurrencies like Bitcoin and Ethereum and smaller, emerging coins. This approach spreads risk across different assets, so if one cryptocurrency performs poorly, others might do well.

It's also essential to **research** each cryptocurrency before investing. Look at the team behind the project, its technology, and its use case. Understanding what you're investing in can help you make better decisions. For example, Bitcoin is often considered a digital store of value, while Ethereum is known for its smart contract functionality. Each cryptocurrency has its unique attributes and potential use cases.

Regularly reviewing and rebalancing your portfolio is also important. As the market changes, some assets might perform better than others, and you might need to adjust your holdings to maintain your desired level of risk and return. Rebalancing involves buying or selling assets to keep your portfolio aligned with your investment goals. This practice helps lock in gains from high-performing investments and reinvest in underperforming ones with growth potential.

Consider setting a **target allocation** for each cryptocurrency in your portfolio. For example, you might decide to allocate 50% of your crypto investments to Bitcoin, 30% to Ethereum, and the remaining 20% to various altcoins. Adjust these allocations based on your risk tolerance and market conditions.

When building your portfolio, think about **diversifying across different sectors** within the cryptocurrency market. For example, you can invest in decentralized finance (DeFi) projects, non-fungible tokens (NFTs), and blockchain infrastructure projects. This sectoral diversification can further reduce risk and expose you to various growth opportunities.

It's also important to have a **long-term perspective**. Cryptocurrency markets can be volatile in the short term, but many projects have shown significant growth over several years. By maintaining a long-term outlook, you can better withstand market fluctuations and focus on the overall growth potential of your investments.

Lastly, keep an emergency fund separate from your crypto investments. This fund should cover essential expenses and provide a financial cushion in case of unexpected events. Relying solely on volatile investments for financial security can be risky, so having a diversified portfolio that includes traditional assets is crucial.

Percentage of Investment Portfolio in Crypto

When deciding how much of your investment portfolio to allocate to cryptocurrency, it's important to consider your risk tolerance and investment goals. Financial experts often recommend that beginners start with a small percentage, such as 1-5% of their total investment portfolio, due to the high volatility and risk associated with cryptocurrencies. More experienced investors who understand the market better might allocate a higher percentage, such as 10-20%.

It's essential to diversify within your crypto holdings and across other asset classes like stocks, bonds, and real estate. This diversification helps protect your overall wealth and reduces the risk of significant losses in any single market. By spreading your investments across different asset classes, you can balance potential gains from cryptocurrencies with the stability of traditional investments.

Consider your overall **investment strategy** when determining the percentage to allocate to crypto. If you have a high-risk tolerance and are seeking high growth potential, you might allocate more to cryptocurrencies. Conversely, if you are more risk-averse, keeping a smaller portion in crypto can help manage potential losses while still allowing for growth opportunities.

Regularly **review and adjust** your allocation as needed. The cryptocurrency market evolves rapidly, and your investment strategy should adapt to changes in market conditions, regulations, and your financial situation. Periodic reviews can help ensure that your portfolio remains aligned with your goals and risk tolerance.

Education is key to making informed decisions about your crypto investments. Stay updated on market trends, technological developments, and regulatory news. The more you understand the cryptocurrency landscape, the better equipped you will be to make strategic investment decisions.

Remember that **long-term growth** often requires patience and discipline. Avoid making impulsive decisions based on short-term market movements. Instead, focus on your long-term investment goals and maintain a diversified portfolio that can weather market volatility.

Diversification Tips

Diversification is a key strategy in managing investment risk. In addition to holding various cryptocurrencies, consider spreading your investments across different sectors of the crypto market. For example, you might invest in coins related to DeFi (Decentralized Finance), gaming, or supply chain management.

Investing in both **stablecoins** and more volatile cryptocurrencies can also help balance risk. Stablecoins are tied to traditional currencies like the US dollar and tend to be less volatile, providing a stable anchor for your portfolio.

It's also wise to diversify outside the cryptocurrency market. Consider investing in traditional assets like stocks, bonds, or real estate. This broader diversification helps protect your overall wealth from the volatility of any single market.

Geographic diversification can also be beneficial. Investing in cryptocurrencies and projects from different regions can reduce the impact of localized economic issues and regulatory changes. This approach ensures that your investments are not overly dependent on the economic and regulatory environment of a single country.

Project diversification within the crypto space is crucial as well. Don't just focus on one type of blockchain technology or application. Spread your investments across various projects, such as smart contract platforms, decentralized applications, and digital identity solutions. This way, you can benefit from the growth of different sectors within the crypto ecosystem.

Lastly, consider **risk management strategies** like stop-loss orders and portfolio insurance. Stop-loss orders can automatically sell a portion of your holdings if the price drops below a certain level, protecting you from significant losses. Portfolio insurance, such as options and futures, can also hedge against adverse market movements.

SUMMARY

Investing in cryptocurrency involves a variety of strategies, each carrying its own set of risks, rewards, and time commitments. Whether you prefer buying and holding, actively trading, staking assets for passive income, or practicing dollar-cost averaging, your approach should align with your financial goals, risk tolerance, and investment timeline.

The popular term **HODL**, originally born from a simple typo, has evolved into a powerful philosophy in the crypto world. It underscores the value of long-term thinking, especially during periods of extreme market volatility. Many seasoned investors have found success not by reacting emotionally to short-term price swings but by sticking to their convictions and holding through the ups and downs.

Building a diversified crypto portfolio is equally important for managing risk. By spreading investments across different cryptocurrencies, sectors (such as DeFi, NFTs, and blockchain infrastructure), and even regions, investors can protect themselves against the failure of any single asset or project. Regular portfolio reviews and rebalancing are essential practices to maintain your desired risk level, lock in gains, and adjust to evolving market conditions.

While the potential rewards in the cryptocurrency market can be substantial, offering opportunities for significant growth and wealth building, the risks are just as real. Volatility, security breaches, regulatory changes, and market manipulation are all realities investors must face. Understanding these risks before you invest can help you prepare for the emotional and financial challenges that come with them.

Most financial experts recommend that cryptocurrency should make up only a **small portion of your overall investment portfolio**. Beginners are generally advised to allocate between **1% to 5%**, while more experienced and risk-tolerant investors might choose to allocate up to **10% to 20%**. No matter how exciting the market appears, it's critical to **only invest what you can afford to lose**. It's wiser to start conservatively, learn by doing, and expand your investment over time as your confidence and understanding of the market grow.

Finally, always remember that success in cryptocurrency investing often depends as much on your **mindset** as on your market timing. Patience, discipline, continuous learning, and emotional resilience are key traits of successful investors in this high-risk, high-reward space.

Important: This chapter is intended to provide general information and should not be considered financial or investment advice. Always conduct thorough research and seek professional guidance tailored to your unique financial situation before making any investment decisions. – *Charles E Tyler*

QUOTE

"Investing in cryptocurrency can be incredibly rewarding, but it's essential to do your homework and understand the risks involved."

– Brian Armstrong, CEO of Coinbase

DEFINITIONS

1. **Buying and Holding**: An investment strategy where you buy assets and hold them for a long period, expecting their value to increase.

2. **Trading**: The practice of buying and selling assets frequently to take advantage of short-term price movements.

3. **Dollar-Cost Averaging (DCA)**: Investing a fixed amount of money at regular intervals, regardless of the asset's price, to reduce the impact of market volatility.

4. **Staking**: Holding cryptocurrencies in a wallet to support network operations and earn rewards.

5. **HODL**: A term originating from a typo, now meaning to hold onto cryptocurrency investments long-term despite market fluctuations.

6. **Volatility**: The degree of variation in the price of an asset over time, indicating its risk level.

7. **Stablecoin**: A type of cryptocurrency that is pegged to a traditional currency, reducing its price volatility.

QUIZ: CHAPTER 4

Investing in Cryptocurrency

1. **What is the buy and hold strategy in cryptocurrency investing?**

    a) Buying cryptocurrency and selling it the next day

    b) Buying cryptocurrency and holding it for a long time, hoping its value will increase

    c) Trading cryptocurrencies daily for quick profits

    d) Only investing in stablecoins for safety

2. **What does HODL stand for, and what does it mean?**

    a) "Hold On for Dear Life" — Keeping cryptocurrency investments long-term despite market volatility

    b) "Help Others Discover Learning" — Teaching others about crypto

    c) "Hold Over Decentralized Ledger" — A blockchain-specific term

    d) "Hide Old Digital Loans" — A banking concept

3. **What are the risks associated with investing in cryptocurrency?**

    a) Guaranteed losses

    b) Volatility, security risks, regulatory uncertainty, and market manipulation

    c) Low returns compared to traditional stocks

    d) Government insurance against losses

4. How can diversification help manage investment risks in cryptocurrency?

    a) By investing only in one popular coin

    b) By investing in many assets across crypto sectors and traditional markets to balance risks and gains

    c) By converting all crypto into fiat currency immediately

    d) By staking only stablecoins

5. What percentage of your investment portfolio should beginners consider allocating to cryptocurrency?

    a) 50-60%

    b) 1-5%

    c) 20-30%

    d) 70-80%

6. What is dollar-cost averaging, and how does it work?

    a) Investing only when crypto prices are low

    b) Investing large sums in one purchase to catch big gains

    c) Investing a fixed amount at regular intervals, regardless of the price, to manage volatility

    d) Waiting for news events before buying

7. What are stablecoins, and why might they be included in a diversified portfolio?

    a) Cryptocurrencies tied to traditional currencies, providing a stable value to reduce overall portfolio volatility

    b) Coins that grow rapidly and guarantee profits

    c) Government-issued crypto assets

    d) Coins used only for paying transaction fees

☑ ANSWER KEY WITH DETAILED EXPLANATIONS

1. b) Buying cryptocurrency and holding it for a long time, hoping its value will increase

    Explanation:

    The "buy and hold" strategy is about staying invested over time, regardless of market ups and downs, aiming for long-term growth.

2. a) "Hold On for Dear Life" — Keeping cryptocurrency investments long-term despite market volatility

    Explanation:

    HODL originated from a typo and symbolizes the mindset of not panicking during crypto market fluctuations.

3. b) Volatility, security risks, regulatory uncertainty, and market manipulation

    Explanation:

    These are major risks discussed in the chapter that investors must consider and manage carefully.

4. b) By investing in many assets across crypto sectors and traditional markets to balance risks and gains

    Explanation:

    Diversification spreads investments, reducing the impact if one asset or sector performs poorly.

5. **b) 1-5%**

   Explanation:

   Because of the high volatility of cryptocurrencies, beginners are advised to limit their exposure to a small portion of their overall portfolio.

6. **c) Investing a fixed amount at regular intervals, regardless of the price, to manage volatility**

   Explanation:

   Dollar-cost averaging reduces the risk of investing a large amount at the wrong time by smoothing out purchases over time.

7. **a) Cryptocurrencies tied to traditional currencies, providing a stable value to reduce overall portfolio volatility**

   Explanation:

   Stablecoins act as an anchor in a crypto portfolio, offering less price fluctuation compared to other crypto assets.

CHAPTER 5

CRYPTOCURRENCY AND ETFs

Key Points

- Introduction to ETFs
- How Crypto ETFs Work
- Benefits and Risks of Crypto ETFs
- Choosing the Right ETF

CONTENT

Introduction to ETFs

An **Exchange-Traded Fund (ETF)** is a type of investment fund that holds a collection of assets like stocks, bonds, or commodities. ETFs are traded on stock exchanges, much like individual stocks. They provide investors with a way to diversify their portfolios without needing to buy each asset individually.

ETFs have become popular due to their flexibility, liquidity, and lower costs compared to mutual funds. They allow investors to gain exposure to a broad range of assets or a specific sector of the market with a single investment. ETFs can track various indices, sectors, or themes, making them versatile investment tools.

ETFs are also known for their tax efficiency. Because they are traded like stocks, investors can buy and sell ETF shares without triggering capital gains taxes until the shares are sold. This can result in lower tax liabilities compared to mutual funds, which might distribute capital gains to investors throughout the year.

With the rise of cryptocurrencies, new types of ETFs have emerged, known as **Crypto ETFs**. These funds aim to provide investors with exposure to the cryptocurrency market without needing to buy and store the digital assets themselves. Crypto ETFs can hold various cryptocurrencies, blockchain-related stocks, or futures contracts.

Crypto ETFs are appealing to investors who are interested in the potential of cryptocurrencies but are wary of the complexities and risks associated with directly owning digital assets. By investing in Crypto ETFs, investors can gain exposure to the cryptocurrency market through a regulated and familiar investment vehicle.

How Crypto ETFs Work

Crypto ETFs operate similarly to traditional ETFs but focus on digital assets and related companies. There are different types of Crypto ETFs:

1. **Direct Cryptocurrency ETFs**: These ETFs hold actual cryptocurrencies like Bitcoin or Ethereum. The fund buys and stores the digital assets, and the value of the ETF shares reflects the price of the

underlying cryptocurrencies. This type of ETF provides direct exposure to the price movements of the cryptocurrencies it holds.

2. **Futures-Based Crypto ETFs**: Instead of holding the actual cryptocurrencies, these ETFs invest in futures contracts. Futures are agreements to buy or sell an asset at a future date for a predetermined price. Futures-based ETFs aim to track the price movements of cryptocurrencies through these contracts. This approach allows investors to gain exposure to the cryptocurrency market without the need for physical custody of the digital assets.

3. **Blockchain ETFs**: These funds invest in companies involved in the blockchain industry, such as technology providers, miners, and other related businesses. While not directly holding cryptocurrencies, they provide exposure to the growth and development of the blockchain ecosystem. Blockchain ETFs can include a mix of established tech companies and smaller, innovative firms driving blockchain adoption.

4. **Hybrid ETFs**: Some ETFs combine different approaches, holding both cryptocurrencies and blockchain-related stocks or futures contracts. This hybrid approach aims to balance the risks and benefits of direct and indirect exposure to the crypto market. Hybrid ETFs can offer diversified exposure to the broader cryptocurrency and blockchain sectors.

Investors can buy and sell shares of Crypto ETFs on stock exchanges, just like traditional ETFs. This makes it easier to gain exposure to cryptocurrencies without dealing with the complexities of buying, storing, and securing digital assets. Crypto ETFs also provide a way to invest in the cryptocurrency market through tax-advantaged accounts like IRAs and 401(k)s.

Benefits and Risks of Crypto ETFs

Crypto ETFs offer several benefits to investors:

1. **Accessibility**: Crypto ETFs make it easier for investors to gain exposure to cryptocurrencies without needing to understand the technical aspects of buying and storing digital assets. This accessibility can attract a broader range of investors, including those who are new to cryptocurrencies.

2. **Diversification**: By holding a basket of assets, Crypto ETFs provide diversification within the cryptocurrency market and related industries. This can reduce the risk associated with investing in a single asset. Diversification helps spread risk across different cryptocurrencies and blockchain-related companies, potentially stabilizing returns.

3. **Liquidity**: ETFs are traded on stock exchanges, offering high liquidity. Investors can buy and sell ETF shares during market hours, providing flexibility in managing their investments. This liquidity is crucial in the often-volatile cryptocurrency market, where prices can change rapidly.

4. **Regulation**: Crypto ETFs are subject to regulatory oversight, providing a level of security and transparency that might be lacking in direct cryptocurrency investments. Regulatory oversight can help protect investors from fraud and ensure that the ETFs operate in a fair and transparent manner.

However, Crypto ETFs also come with risks:

1. **Market Volatility**: Cryptocurrencies are known for their high volatility, and this can lead to significant price fluctuations in Crypto ETFs. Investors must be prepared for potential rapid changes in

value. While diversification can mitigate some risk, the inherent volatility of cryptocurrencies remains a factor.

2. **Management Fees**: ETFs charge management fees, which can vary. These fees can reduce overall returns, especially if the ETF does not perform well. Investors should compare the fees of different Crypto ETFs and consider their impact on long-term returns.

3. **Regulatory Changes**: The regulatory environment for cryptocurrencies is still evolving. New regulations can impact the performance and availability of Crypto ETFs. Regulatory changes can affect the underlying assets, the operation of the ETFs, and investor sentiment towards cryptocurrencies.

4. **Tracking Errors**: Some ETFs might not perfectly track the price movements of the underlying assets, leading to discrepancies between the ETF's performance and the actual price of the cryptocurrencies or blockchain stocks. Tracking errors can result from various factors, including management decisions, market conditions, and the structure of the ETF.

Choosing the Right ETF

When choosing a Crypto ETF, investors should consider several factors:

1. **Underlying Assets**: Understand what assets the ETF holds. Does it invest in actual cryptocurrencies, futures contracts, or blockchain-related stocks? Knowing this can help align the investment with your goals and risk tolerance. For example, a direct cryptocurrency ETF might be more suitable for investors seeking pure crypto exposure, while a blockchain ETF might appeal to those interested in the broader industry.

2. **Management Fees**: Compare the fees charged by different ETFs. Higher fees can eat into your returns, so look for funds with reasonable costs. Management fees are typically expressed as an expense ratio, which is the annual fee charged as a percentage of the fund's assets.

3. **Performance History**: Review the historical performance of the ETF. While past performance is not indicative of future results, it can provide insights into how the ETF has managed market volatility and other challenges. Look at performance over various time frames and compare it to relevant benchmarks.

4. **Liquidity**: Ensure the ETF is actively traded with sufficient liquidity. High liquidity allows for easier buying and selling of shares without significantly impacting the price. ETFs with higher trading volumes tend to have narrower bid-ask spreads, reducing transaction costs for investors.

5. **Regulatory Environment**: Stay informed about the regulatory landscape for cryptocurrencies and Crypto ETFs. Regulatory changes can affect the performance and availability of these investment products. Understanding the regulatory environment can help investors anticipate potential risks and opportunities.

6. **Issuer Reputation**: Consider the reputation of the ETF issuer. Established and reputable issuers are more likely to offer well-managed and secure investment products. Research the issuer's history, financial strength, and experience in managing ETFs.

Investing in Crypto ETFs can provide a convenient and diversified way to gain exposure to the cryptocurrency market. By carefully considering the underlying assets, fees, performance, liquidity, regulatory environment, and issuer reputation, investors can choose the right ETF that aligns with their investment goals and risk tolerance.

ADDITIONAL INSIGHTS

Important Note:

This chapter is intended for **informational purposes only** and should not be considered investment advice. Always consult a licensed financial advisor before making investment decisions.

⊞ Info Box: Examples of Popular Crypto ETFs

- **ProShares Bitcoin Strategy ETF (BITO):**
- Focuses on Bitcoin futures contracts, offering exposure without direct Bitcoin ownership.
- **Grayscale Bitcoin Trust (GBTC):**
- A trust that provides indirect Bitcoin exposure, widely traded but structured differently than traditional ETFs.
- **Valkyrie Bitcoin Strategy ETF (BTF):**
- Another Bitcoin futures ETF designed for investors using traditional brokerage accounts.
- **Bitwise Crypto Industry Innovators ETF (BITQ):**
- Invests in companies driving innovation in the crypto and blockchain sectors.

📝 *Note: Always research each ETF's structure, management fees, and risks before investing. Past performance does not guarantee future results.*

A Quick Word About Leverage

Some Crypto ETFs use **leverage**, meaning they borrow money to amplify returns. While this can boost gains in a rising market, it can also **magnify losses** just as quickly.

Leverage adds another layer of risk and may not be suitable for all investors, especially those new to cryptocurrency investing.

Who Should Consider Investing in Crypto ETFs?

Crypto ETFs may appeal to investors who:

- Want exposure to the cryptocurrency market without handling digital wallets or private keys.
- Prefer using traditional brokerage accounts like IRAs, 401(k)s, or standard brokerage accounts.
- Are interested in regulated investment vehicles but accept cryptocurrency market volatility.
- Seek diversification in the blockchain and digital asset sectors without picking individual coins.

Investors should always evaluate their **risk tolerance, investment goals**, and **time horizon** carefully before investing.

SUMMARY

Crypto ETFs offer a convenient way for investors to gain exposure to the cryptocurrency market without the technical challenges of buying, storing, and securing digital assets. These investment funds can hold actual cryptocurrencies, invest in futures contracts, or focus on companies involved in the blockchain industry. Crypto ETFs provide key benefits like accessibility, diversification, liquidity, and regulatory oversight, making them an attractive option for many investors.

However, Crypto ETFs also carry risks, including high market volatility, management fees, regulatory uncertainties, and the possibility of tracking errors. Some ETFs may even use leverage, which can amplify both gains and losses, adding another layer of risk that investors should carefully consider.

Choosing the right Crypto ETF requires understanding what the fund holds, comparing management fees, reviewing historical performance, evaluating liquidity, monitoring the evolving regulatory environment, and considering the issuer's reputation. Popular examples like the ProShares Bitcoin Strategy ETF (BITO) and the Grayscale Bitcoin Trust (GBTC) show the variety of ways investors can access this space.

Crypto ETFs may be a good fit for those who want crypto exposure through traditional brokerage accounts and prefer regulated, familiar investment vehicles. As with any investment, aligning choices with personal goals, risk tolerance, and time horizon is essential.

Important: This chapter is for informational purposes only and does not constitute investment advice. Always conduct your own research or consult with a licensed financial professional before investing.

QUOTE

"Investing in crypto ETFs offers a way to gain exposure to the cryptocurrency market with the added benefits of regulation, diversification, and liquidity."

– Cathie Wood, CEO of ARK Invest

DEFINITIONS

1. **ETF (Exchange-Traded Fund)**: A type of investment fund that holds a collection of assets like stocks, bonds, or commodities and is traded on stock exchanges.

2. **Crypto ETF**: An ETF that provides exposure to the cryptocurrency market by holding cryptocurrencies, futures contracts, or blockchain-related stocks.

3. **Futures Contract**: An agreement to buy or sell an asset at a future date for a predetermined price.

4. **Blockchain ETF**: An ETF that invests in companies involved in the blockchain industry, providing indirect exposure to cryptocurrencies.

5. **Liquidity**: The ease with which an asset can be bought or sold in the market without affecting its price.

6. **Management Fees**: Fees charged by ETF issuers for managing the fund, which can impact overall returns.

7. **Tracking Error**: The difference between the performance of an ETF and the performance of its underlying assets.

QUIZ: CHAPTER 5

Cryptocurrency and ETFs

1. What is a primary advantage of investing in a Crypto ETF instead of directly buying cryptocurrencies?

    a) Higher returns

    b) Guaranteed profits

    c) Exposure to the crypto market without managing digital assets directly

    d) Lower risk compared to government bonds

2. Which type of Crypto ETF invests in agreements to buy or sell an asset at a future date for a predetermined price?

    a) Blockchain ETF

    b) Direct Cryptocurrency ETF

    c) Hybrid ETF

    d) Futures-Based Crypto ETF

3. Which of the following is NOT listed as a major risk of investing in Crypto ETFs?

    a) Market Volatility

    b) Management Fees

    c) Guaranteed returns

    d) Regulatory Changes

4. **When choosing a Crypto ETF, why is it important to consider the issuer's reputation?**

   a) To ensure the ETF pays dividends

   b) To make sure the ETF is well-managed and secure

   c) To guarantee rapid price increases

   d) To avoid investing in traditional stocks

5. **What does the term "liquidity" mean in the context of Crypto ETFs?**

   a) The level of regulation of the ETF

   b) The ease of buying or selling ETF shares without affecting their price

   c) The stability of cryptocurrency prices

   d) The number of cryptocurrencies held by the ETF

6. **Which popular Crypto ETF focuses on Bitcoin futures contracts?**

   a) Grayscale Bitcoin Trust (GBTC)

   b) Bitwise Crypto Industry Innovators ETF (BITQ)

   c) ProShares Bitcoin Strategy ETF (BITO)

   d) Valkyrie Blockchain Innovators ETF

☑ ANSWER KEY WITH DETAILED EXPLANATIONS

1. c) Exposure to the crypto market without managing digital assets directly

   Explanation:

   Crypto ETFs allow investors to gain exposure to cryptocurrencies without needing to buy, store, or secure digital assets like Bitcoin or Ethereum. This offers a simpler, more regulated way to participate in the crypto market.

2. d) Futures-Based Crypto ETF

   Explanation:

   Futures-Based Crypto ETFs invest in contracts to buy or sell cryptocurrency at a future date for a set price. These funds don't hold the actual crypto but aim to track its price through futures agreements.

3. c) Guaranteed returns

   Explanation:

   There are no guaranteed returns with Crypto ETFs. Risks such as market volatility, management fees, and regulatory changes can affect performance. Believing that any crypto investment offers guaranteed profits is a common misconception.

4. b) To make sure the ETF is well-managed and secure

   Explanation:

   A reputable ETF issuer is more likely to offer secure, professionally managed products. Choosing a trustworthy issuer helps reduce risk and ensures that the ETF is operated properly.

5. **b) The ease of buying or selling ETF shares without affecting their price**

    Explanation:

    Liquidity refers to how easily an investor can buy or sell shares of an ETF. High liquidity means trades can be made quickly without affecting the price too much, which is especially important in volatile markets.

6. **c) ProShares Bitcoin Strategy ETF (BITO)**

    Explanation:

    The ProShares Bitcoin Strategy ETF (BITO) offers exposure to Bitcoin by investing in futures contracts. It allows investors to participate in Bitcoin price movements without directly holding the asset.

CHAPTER 6

THE IMPACT OF CRYPTO AND BLOCKCHAIN ON FINANCE

Key Points

- Decentralized Finance (DeFi)
- Cryptocurrencies as Investments
- Regulatory Landscape
- Traditional Finance vs. Crypto Finance

CONTENT

Decentralized Finance (DeFi)

Decentralized Finance (DeFi) is a revolutionary concept that leverages blockchain technology to recreate and improve traditional financial systems. DeFi aims to eliminate intermediaries like banks and brokers, providing financial services directly through decentralized applications (dApps). These services include lending, borrowing, trading, and earning interest on digital assets.

One of the primary advantages of DeFi is increased accessibility. Traditional financial systems often exclude individuals without access to banking infrastructure. DeFi platforms, however, are accessible to anyone with an internet connection and a digital wallet, democratizing financial services globally.

DeFi platforms operate through smart contracts, which are self-executing contracts with the terms of the agreement directly written into code. This eliminates the need for a trusted third party, reducing costs and increasing transaction speed. For example, platforms like Aave and Compound allow users to lend and borrow cryptocurrencies directly from each other, earning interest or paying it, all governed by smart contracts.

Another significant benefit of DeFi is transparency. All transactions on DeFi platforms are recorded on a public blockchain, making them auditable and traceable. This transparency can reduce fraud and corruption, as all activities are visible and verifiable.

However, DeFi also comes with risks. The reliance on smart contracts introduces technical risks, as bugs or vulnerabilities in the code can lead to significant financial losses. Additionally, the regulatory environment for DeFi is still developing, and future regulations could impact the growth and operation of DeFi platforms.

Cryptocurrencies as Investments

Cryptocurrencies have emerged as a popular investment class, attracting both individual and institutional investors. Bitcoin, often referred to as digital gold, is seen as a store of value and a hedge against inflation. Its limited supply and decentralized nature make it an attractive alternative to traditional assets like gold.

Ethereum, the second-largest cryptocurrency by market capitalization, offers more than just a store of value. Its blockchain supports smart contracts and decentralized applications, providing utility beyond a mere digital currency. This has led to the rise of various tokens built on the Ethereum platform, each with unique use cases and investment potentials.

Investing in cryptocurrencies offers the potential for high returns, as demonstrated by the significant price increases of major cryptocurrencies over the past decade. However, this potential comes with high volatility. Cryptocurrency prices can fluctuate dramatically in short periods, driven by market sentiment, regulatory news, technological developments, and macroeconomic trends.

Institutional adoption of cryptocurrencies is growing. Companies like Tesla, MicroStrategy, and Square have invested in Bitcoin, and financial institutions are increasingly offering cryptocurrency services to their clients. This adoption can provide more stability to the market and increase the legitimacy of cryptocurrencies as an investment class.

However, investing in cryptocurrencies also requires caution. The market is still relatively young and can be subject to manipulation and fraud. It's crucial for investors to conduct thorough research, understand the risks, and only invest what they can afford to lose.

Regulatory Landscape

The regulatory environment for cryptocurrencies and blockchain technology is complex and constantly evolving. Different countries have varying approaches to regulation, ranging from supportive to restrictive. Understanding these regulations is crucial for both users and investors.

In the United States, regulatory bodies like the Securities and Exchange Commission (SEC), the Commodity Futures Trading Commission (CFTC), and the Financial Crimes Enforcement Network (FinCEN) oversee different aspects of the cryptocurrency market. The SEC, for example, focuses on whether cryptocurrencies are considered securities and thus subject to securities laws. The CFTC regulates cryptocurrency derivatives, while FinCEN enforces anti-money laundering (AML) regulations.

The European Union has taken steps to create a unified regulatory framework for cryptocurrencies. The proposed Markets in Crypto-Assets (MiCA) regulation aims to provide legal clarity and protect investors while fostering innovation. It covers various aspects, including the issuance and trading of cryptocurrencies and the operation of crypto-asset service providers.

In contrast, some countries have taken a more restrictive approach. China, for example, has banned cryptocurrency trading and mining activities, citing concerns about financial stability and environmental impact. India has also considered strict regulations, although the legal status of cryptocurrencies remains uncertain.

Regulatory developments can significantly impact the cryptocurrency market. Positive regulations can enhance market confidence and encourage adoption, while restrictive measures can lead to market downturns and reduced innovation. Staying informed about regulatory changes and understanding their implications is essential for anyone involved in the cryptocurrency spaceTraditional Finance vs. Crypto Finance

The rise of cryptocurrencies and blockchain technology has led to a clash between traditional finance (TradFi) and crypto finance. Each system has its strengths and weaknesses, and understanding these differences is crucial for navigating the financial landscape.

Traditional finance relies on established institutions like banks, brokerages, and payment processors. These institutions provide a wide range of financial services, including savings accounts, loans, investments, and payment processing. They are regulated by government bodies, ensuring a level of stability and consumer protection.

Crypto finance, on the other hand, operates on decentralized networks using blockchain technology. It aims to provide similar financial services without intermediaries, relying on smart contracts and decentralized applications. This can reduce costs, increase accessibility, and enhance transparency.

One significant advantage of traditional finance is its stability and trust. Banks and financial institutions have established reputations and are subject to rigorous regulatory oversight. Consumers have legal protections, such as deposit insurance, that are not typically available in the crypto space.

However, traditional finance can also be slow, expensive, and exclusionary. Transactions can take days to settle, fees can be high, and millions of people globally lack access to basic banking services. Crypto finance aims to address these issues by providing faster, cheaper, and more inclusive financial services.

The integration of crypto finance into the traditional financial system is already underway. Major financial institutions are exploring blockchain technology for various applications, such as cross-border payments and supply chain finance. Additionally, the rise of stablecoins, which are digital currencies pegged to traditional assets like the US dollar, bridges the gap between crypto and traditional finance.

Understanding the differences and potential synergies between traditional finance and crypto finance can help individuals and businesses make informed decisions about their financial strategies.

SUMMARY

The impact of crypto and blockchain on finance is profound and far-reaching. Decentralized Finance (DeFi) offers innovative financial services without intermediaries, increasing accessibility and transparency. Cryptocurrencies have emerged as a new investment class, attracting both individual and institutional investors, though they come with high volatility and regulatory challenges. The regulatory landscape for cryptocurrencies is complex and evolving, with different countries taking varying approaches. The rise of crypto finance challenges traditional financial systems but also presents opportunities for integration and improvement. Understanding these dynamics is essential for navigating the future of finance.

QUOTE

"Blockchain is the biggest opportunity set we can think of over the next decade or so."

– Bob Greifeld, former CEO of NASDAQ

DEFINITIONS

1. **Decentralized Finance (DeFi)**: A financial system built on blockchain technology that operates without traditional financial intermediaries like banks. DeFi allows for peer-to-peer financial transactions and services such as lending, borrowing, and trading through decentralized applications (dApps).

2. **Automated Market Maker (AMM)**: A type of decentralized exchange protocol that relies on a mathematical formula to price assets, allowing for automated and permissionless trading of cryptocurrency pairs without traditional order books.

3. **Yield Farming**: A practice in DeFi where users provide liquidity to protocols and earn rewards, typically in the form of interest or additional cryptocurrency, as an incentive for participating in the network.

4. **Flash Loan**: A type of uncollateralized loan available in DeFi that must be borrowed and repaid within a single transaction block, often used for arbitrage, refinancing, or other trading strategies.

5. **Tokenization**: The process of converting ownership rights or assets into digital tokens on a blockchain, making them more easily tradable and divisible.

6. **Oracle**: A service that provides external data to smart contracts on a blockchain, enabling them to execute based on real-world events or conditions.

7. **Liquidity Pool**: A collection of funds locked in a smart contract that provides liquidity for decentralized trading platforms, allowing users to trade assets without the need for a traditional order book.

QUIZ

The Impact of Crypto and Blockchain on Finance

1. **What is Decentralized Finance (DeFi)?**

   a) A centralized banking system using blockchain

   b) A financial system that eliminates intermediaries by using blockchain and smart contracts

   c) A payment app for traditional currencies

   d) A government-issued cryptocurrency network

2. **What are the main benefits of investing in cryptocurrencies?**

   a) Guaranteed returns and low taxes

   b) Easy access to government bonds

   c) Potential for high returns, diversification, and increased accessibility

   d) Automatic deposit insurance by banks

3. **What are some risks associated with DeFi platforms?**

   a) Stable market prices and low transaction fees

   b) Technical vulnerabilities, regulatory uncertainty, and potential financial losses

   c) Guaranteed interest rates

   d) Unlimited government backing

4. **How do traditional finance and crypto finance differ?**

   a) Both rely heavily on centralized regulators

   b) Traditional finance uses banks and intermediaries, while crypto finance operates through decentralized networks without middlemen

   c) Crypto finance has longer transaction settlement times

   d) Traditional finance allows anonymous transactions like crypto finance

5. **Why is understanding the regulatory landscape important for cryptocurrency investors?**

   a) It helps investors avoid using blockchain networks altogether

   b) Regulatory changes can influence the legality, performance, and adoption of cryptocurrencies

   c) It ensures that cryptocurrencies stay tax-free

   d) Regulation guarantees that all cryptocurrencies will be profitable

6. **What role do smart contracts play in DeFi?**

   a) They allow governments to regulate blockchains remotely

   b) They automate financial transactions and agreements without intermediaries, increasing transparency and efficiency

   c) They manually process crypto loans

   d) They eliminate the need for blockchain technology altogether

☑ ANSWER KEY WITH DETAILED EXPLANATIONS

1. **b) A financial system that eliminates intermediaries by using block-chain and smart contracts**

   Explanation:

   DeFi removes the need for traditional banks and brokers by using decentralized applications and smart contracts to deliver financial services directly.

2. **c) Potential for high returns, diversification, and increased accessibility**

   Explanation:

   Cryptocurrencies offer investors the opportunity for significant returns, diversify traditional portfolios, and open investment opportunities globally without banking barriers.

3. **b) Technical vulnerabilities, regulatory uncertainty, and potential financial losses**

   Explanation:

   DeFi platforms rely heavily on smart contracts, which can be exploited if poorly coded, and regulatory shifts could heavily impact platform operation or legality.

4. **b) Traditional finance uses banks and intermediaries, while crypto finance operates through decentralized networks without middlemen**

   Explanation:

   Traditional systems rely on centralized oversight and service providers, while crypto finance uses peer-to-peer networks and smart contracts to reduce costs and increase efficiency.

5. b) Regulatory changes can influence the legality, performance, and adoption of cryptocurrencies

Explanation:

Positive regulations can boost investor confidence and innovation, while negative or unclear regulations can cause market downturns or limit crypto development.

6. b) They automate financial transactions and agreements without intermediaries, increasing transparency and efficiency

Explanation:

Smart contracts ensure that transactions execute only when conditions are met, eliminating the need for banks or lawyers in many DeFi scenarios.

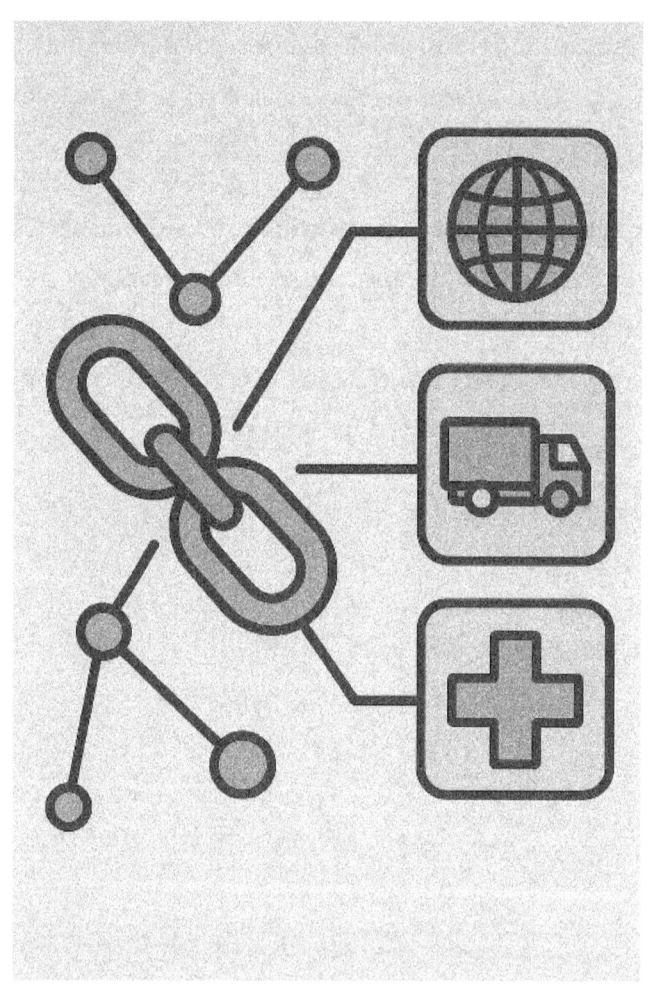

CHAPTER 7

REAL-WORLD APPLICATIONS OF BLOCKCHAIN

Key Points

- Supply Chain Management
- Healthcare and Data Security
- Voting Systems and Governance
- Real Estate and Property Management

CONTENT

Supply Chain Management

Blockchain technology has the potential to revolutionize supply chain management by increasing transparency, traceability, and efficiency. In traditional supply chains, tracking the movement of goods from origin to destination can be complex and prone to errors and fraud. Blockchain provides a decentralized and immutable ledger where all participants in the supply chain can record and verify transactions.

For example, IBM's Food Trust blockchain is used by companies like Walmart and Nestlé to track the journey of food products from farms to store shelves. By scanning QR codes on products, consumers can access detailed information about the product's origin, processing, and journey through the supply chain. This enhances food safety by quickly identifying and isolating contaminated products, reducing the risk of foodborne illnesses.

Moreover, blockchain can streamline administrative processes in supply chains. Smart contracts can automate tasks such as payments and compliance checks, reducing delays and costs. When a shipment reaches a certain location, the smart contract can automatically release payment to the supplier, ensuring timely transactions without the need for intermediaries.

Despite these benefits, the adoption of blockchain in supply chain management faces challenges. Integrating blockchain with existing systems, ensuring data accuracy, and achieving industry-wide standards requires significant effort and collaboration. However, as technology matures and adoption increases, these challenges are likely to diminish.

Healthcare and Data Security

In healthcare, blockchain technology offers solutions for improving data security, interoperability, and patient care. The healthcare industry faces significant challenges in managing patient records, ensuring data privacy, and enabling secure data sharing among providers.

Blockchain can provide a secure and tamper-proof system for storing and sharing patient records. Each patient can have a unique identifier on the blockchain, allowing authorized healthcare providers to access and update records securely. This reduces the risk of data breaches and ensures that patients' medical histories are accurate and up-to-date.

For example, the Estonian government has implemented a blockchain-based system for securing health records. This system allows patients to control access to their data and enables seamless data sharing between different healthcare providers, improving coordination and care quality.

Additionally, blockchain can enhance the traceability and safety of pharmaceuticals. By recording every step of the production and distribution process on the blockchain, manufacturers and regulators can verify the authenticity of medicines and detect counterfeit products. This can significantly reduce the prevalence of fake drugs, which pose serious health risks.

While blockchain offers many benefits to healthcare, challenges such as regulatory compliance, integration with legacy systems, and ensuring data accuracy need to be addressed. Collaborative efforts between healthcare providers, technology companies, and regulators are essential for realizing the full potential of blockchain in healthcare.

Voting Systems and Governance

Blockchain technology can transform voting systems and governance by enhancing transparency, security, and trust in the electoral process. Traditional voting systems are susceptible to fraud, tampering, and errors, leading to questions about the integrity of election results.

Blockchain-based voting systems offer a secure and transparent alternative. Each vote can be recorded on the blockchain, creating an immutable and verifiable record. Voters can verify that their vote was counted correctly without revealing their identity, ensuring privacy and security.

For example, in 2018, the Swiss city of Zug conducted a blockchain-based municipal vote, allowing residents to participate securely and transparently. The pilot project demonstrated the potential of blockchain to improve the voting process and increase voter confidence.

Blockchain can also facilitate decentralized governance in organizations and communities. Decentralized Autonomous Organizations (DAOs) use smart contracts to enable transparent decision-making and resource management. Members can propose and vote on initiatives, with results automatically recorded on the blockchain, ensuring accountability and reducing the risk of corruption.

Despite its potential, implementing blockchain-based voting systems faces challenges, such as ensuring accessibility for all voters, preventing coercion, and achieving regulatory compliance. Ongoing research and pilot projects are crucial for addressing these challenges and demonstrating the viability of blockchain in voting and governance.

Real Estate and Property Management

Blockchain technology can streamline real estate transactions and property management by reducing fraud, increasing transparency, and simplifying processes. Traditional real estate transactions involve numerous intermediaries, extensive paperwork, and lengthy verification processes.

Blockchain can simplify these transactions by providing a transparent and secure ledger for recording property ownership and transfer. Smart contracts can automate processes such as title transfers, escrow services, and payment releases. This reduces the need for intermediaries, lowers costs, and speeds up transactions.

For example, Propy is a blockchain-based platform that enables real estate transactions to be conducted online. Buyers and sellers can complete the entire transaction process, from listing properties to transferring ownership, using blockchain technology. This increases efficiency and reduces the risk of fraud.

In property management, blockchain can enhance transparency and accountability. Property managers can use blockchain to record rental agreements, maintenance requests, and financial transactions. This creates a verifiable and tamper-proof record, ensuring that all parties adhere to their obligations.

However, the adoption of blockchain in real estate and property management requires addressing challenges such as legal recognition of blockchain records, integration with existing systems, and ensuring data accuracy. Collaboration between industry stakeholders, technology providers, and regulators is essential for overcoming these challenges and realizing the benefits of blockchain.

SUMMARY

Blockchain technology has a wide range of real-world applications, from supply chain management to healthcare, voting systems, and real estate. In supply chain management, blockchain enhances transparency, traceability, and efficiency, while in healthcare, it improves data security and interoperability. Blockchain-based voting systems offer secure and transparent alternatives to traditional voting methods, and in real estate, blockchain simplifies transactions and increases transparency. Despite the challenges, the potential benefits of blockchain across various industries are significant, promising increased efficiency, security, and trust.

QUOTE

"Blockchain is the technology that underpins trust in the digital age."

– Don Tapscott, Author and Blockchain Expert

DEFINITIONS

1. **Decentralized Application (dApp)**: A software application that runs on a decentralized network, typically using blockchain technology, and operates without a central authority.

2. **Smart Contract**: Self-executing contracts with the terms of the agreement directly written into code, running on a blockchain.

3. **Interoperability**: The ability of different systems, devices, or applications to work together and exchange information effectively.

4. **Immutable Ledger**: A record-keeping system where entries, once made, cannot be altered or deleted, ensuring data integrity and transparency.

5. **Tokenization**: The process of converting ownership rights or assets into digital tokens on a blockchain.

6. **Decentralized Autonomous Organization (DAO)**: An organization governed by smart contracts and decentralized voting, operating without centralized control.

QUIZ

Real-World Applications of Blockchain

1. How does blockchain technology improve supply chain management?

    a) By increasing marketing reach

    b) By enhancing transparency, traceability, and efficiency through a decentralized ledger

    c) By reducing the need for inventory management

    d) By eliminating all shipping costs

2. What are the benefits of using blockchain in healthcare?

    a) Better advertising campaigns

    b) Improved data security, interoperability, accurate patient records, and traceability of pharmaceuticals

    c) Faster hospital construction

    d) Reducing patient-doctor communication

3. How can blockchain-based voting systems enhance electoral processes?

    a) By reducing the number of voters

    b) By allowing votes to be altered after submission

    c) By creating immutable and verifiable voting records that increase transparency and security

    d) By increasing election costs

4. **What challenges must be addressed for widespread adoption of blockchain in real estate?**

   a) Marketing issues

   b) Legal recognition, integration with existing systems, and ensuring data accuracy

   c) Increasing transaction taxes

   d) Decreasing property values

5. **What is a Decentralized Autonomous Organization (DAO), and how does it function?**

   a) A government agency for blockchain oversight

   b) A decentralized group governed by smart contracts and member voting without centralized control

   c) A private real estate investment firm

   d) A nonprofit organization promoting internet access

6. **How does tokenization benefit real estate transactions?**

   a) It simplifies transactions, reduces fraud, and increases transparency by converting ownership rights into digital tokens

   b) It inflates property prices artificially

   c) It eliminates the need for property taxes

   d) It allows only banks to manage property transactions

☑ ANSWER KEY WITH DETAILED EXPLANATIONS

1. **b) By enhancing transparency, traceability, and efficiency through a decentralized ledger**

    Explanation:

    Blockchain allows all participants in a supply chain to view, verify, and track transactions securely, reducing fraud, speeding up operations, and making processes more transparent.

2. **b) Improved data security, interoperability, accurate patient records, and traceability of pharmaceuticals**

    Explanation:

    Blockchain strengthens healthcare by securing patient records, improving communication between providers, and tracking pharmaceuticals to prevent counterfeits.

3. **c) By creating immutable and verifiable voting records that increase transparency and security**

    Explanation:

    Blockchain-based voting ensures that votes are securely recorded and cannot be altered, building public trust in the integrity of elections.

4. **b) Legal recognition, integration with existing systems, and ensuring data accuracy**

    Explanation:

    For blockchain to transform real estate, records must be legally recognized, systems must connect smoothly, and accurate data entry must be maintained to ensure trust and efficiency.

5. **b) A decentralized group governed by smart contracts and member voting without centralized control**

   Explanation:

   DAOs operate using blockchain-based rules (smart contracts), allowing communities to make decisions transparently without relying on central authorities.

6. **a) It simplifies transactions, reduces fraud, and increases transparency by converting ownership rights into digital tokens**

   Explanation:

   Tokenization makes buying and selling property faster and safer by digitizing ownership records, cutting out middlemen, and ensuring transparent transactions.

CHAPTER 8

REGULATION AND COMPLIANCE

Key Points

- Global Regulatory Frameworks
- Navigating Legal Challenges
- Future Regulatory Trends
- Impact on Innovation

CONTENT

Global Regulatory Frameworks

The regulation of cryptocurrencies and blockchain technology varies significantly across different countries, reflecting diverse approaches to balancing innovation, consumer protection, and financial stability. In the United States, the regulatory landscape is fragmented, with multiple agencies overseeing different aspects of the cryptocurrency market.

United States: The Securities and Exchange Commission (SEC) is responsible for regulating securities markets in the U.S. Its primary role is to protect investors, maintain fair and efficient markets, and facilitate capital formation. The SEC applies the Howey Test to determine whether a cryptocurrency or token is considered a security. If classified as a security, the cryptocurrency must comply with securities laws, including registration and disclosure requirements. The SEC's actions impact the crypto space significantly by ensuring that Initial Coin Offerings (ICOs) and other crypto offerings are conducted transparently and legally. Recent high-profile cases, such as the lawsuit against Ripple Labs, highlight the SEC's role in enforcing securities regulations in the crypto industry.

The Commodity Futures Trading Commission (CFTC) regulates the U.S. derivatives markets, including futures, swaps, and certain types of options. In the context of cryptocurrencies, the CFTC has declared Bitcoin and Ethereum as commodities and thus falls under its jurisdiction. The CFTC oversees cryptocurrency derivatives markets, ensuring that trading is conducted fairly and transparently. This includes regulating futures contracts and other derivative products based on cryptocurrencies.

The Financial Crimes Enforcement Network (FinCEN) is a bureau of the U.S. Department of the Treasury and focuses on safeguarding the financial system from illicit use, combating money laundering, and promoting national security. FinCEN's Anti-Money Laundering (AML) regulations require cryptocurrency businesses, such as exchanges and wallet providers, to implement robust Know Your Customer (KYC) procedures. These procedures include verifying the identity of customers, monitoring transactions for suspicious activity, and reporting to FinCEN when necessary.

European Union: The European Union is working towards a unified regulatory framework through the proposed Markets in Crypto-Assets (MiCA) regulation. MiCA aims to provide legal clarity, protect investors, and foster innovation by covering various aspects of cryptocurrency issuance and trading, and the operation of crypto-asset service providers. MiCA will create a consistent regulatory environment across EU member states, making it easier for companies to operate throughout the region. Key aspects include mandatory registration for crypto-asset issuers, stringent requirements for stablecoins, and provisions for market abuse and consumer protection.

Japan: Japan has established one of the most progressive regulatory environments for cryptocurrencies. The Financial Services Agency (FSA) oversees the industry, requiring exchanges to register and comply with stringent AML and customer protection measures. The FSA ensures that exchanges implement robust security measures, conduct regular audits, and comply with KYC regulations. Japan's proactive stance has encouraged innovation while ensuring consumer safety. The FSA's regulations have helped Japan become a major hub for cryptocurrency activity, promoting a secure and transparent market.

China: China has taken a stringent approach, implementing a comprehensive ban on cryptocurrency trading and mining. The Chinese government cites concerns over financial stability, fraud, and environmental impact. Despite the ban, China continues to explore the development of its own central bank digital currency (CBDC), the Digital Yuan. CBDCs are digital forms of central bank-issued currency designed to modernize financial systems and provide a digital alternative to traditional cash. The Digital Yuan aims to enhance payment efficiency and reduce the reliance on the traditional banking system. China's regulatory stance impacts the global cryptocurrency market by reducing the influence of Chinese miners and traders.

Singapore: Singapore offers a supportive regulatory environment through the Monetary Authority of Singapore (MAS). MAS has created clear guidelines for cryptocurrency exchanges and token issuances, promoting a safe and innovative market. MAS requires exchanges to register and comply with AML and KYC regulations, ensuring that they operate transparently and securely. Singapore's regulatory framework has attracted many blockchain and fintech companies, fostering growth and innovation in the sector. MAS also encourages public-private partnerships to explore and develop blockchain technology, further strengthening Singapore's position as a global fintech hub.

By understanding these regulatory frameworks, stakeholders in the cryptocurrency industry can better navigate the complex landscape and ensure compliance with relevant laws and regulations. This knowledge is crucial for fostering a secure, innovative, and sustainable crypto market globally.

Navigating Legal Challenges

Navigating the legal landscape of the cryptocurrency market involves understanding and complying with various regulations that differ by jurisdiction. Businesses and investors must be vigilant in adhering to these regulations to avoid legal repercussions.

AML and KYC Regulations: Anti-money laundering (AML) and know-your-customer (KYC) regulations require businesses to verify the identity of their clients to prevent fraud, money laundering, and other illegal activities. This process involves collecting personal information and monitoring transactions for suspicious activity. Compliance with AML and KYC regulations is crucial for cryptocurrency exchanges and service providers to maintain their licenses and operate legally.

Classification of Cryptocurrencies: The classification of cryptocurrencies presents another significant legal challenge. In the U.S., the SEC has classified certain cryptocurrencies as securities, making them subject to securities laws. This classification impacts how these assets can be traded and what disclosures are required. For example, the SEC's lawsuits against Ripple Labs, the company behind XRP, highlight the complexities of cryptocurrency classification and regulation. Ripple is accused of conducting an unregistered securities offering by selling XRP tokens.

The Howey Test: A critical tool in determining whether a cryptocurrency is considered a security is the Howey Test, established by the U.S. Supreme Court in the case SEC v. W.J. Howey Co. (1946). The Howey Test outlines four criteria:

1. An investment of money
2. In a common enterprise
3. With an expectation of profits
4. Derived from the efforts of others

If a transaction meets all four of these criteria, it is deemed a security and subject to relevant regulations. The SEC has applied the Howey Test in its case against Ripple, arguing that the sale of XRP constitutes an investment contract.

Taxation: Taxation is also a critical issue. Different jurisdictions have varying approaches to taxing cryptocurrencies. In the U.S., the IRS treats cryptocurrencies as property, subjecting transactions to capital gains tax. This means that every sale, trade, or even the use of cryptocurrency to purchase goods can create a taxable event. Investors must maintain detailed records of their transactions to ensure accurate tax reporting and compliance.

Intellectual Property Rights: Intellectual property rights in blockchain technology also pose challenges. Blockchain's decentralized nature complicates the enforcement of traditional intellectual property laws. For example, open-source blockchain projects may have difficulty protecting their innovations, while companies developing proprietary solutions must navigate complex patent landscapes.

Recent Legal Issues:

- **Ripple (XRP)**: Ripple Labs has faced legal action from the SEC, which alleges that the company's sale of XRP constitutes an unregistered securities offering. Ripple argues that XRP should not be classified as a security, highlighting the ongoing debate over how cryptocurrencies should be regulated. As of now, the case remains unresolved, with potential implications for the broader cryptocurrency market depending on the outcome. Ripple's CEO, Brad Garlinghouse, remains active in defending the company's position and emphasizing the positive impact of the recent judgment for the industry.

- **FTX**: The cryptocurrency exchange FTX has faced scrutiny over its compliance with AML and KYC regulations. Issues have arisen regarding its operations in different jurisdictions, prompting investigations and legal actions to ensure compliance with local laws. For instance, FTX has been investigated by regulators in the United States and other countries for potential AML violations and operational discrepancies. Former CEO Sam Bankman-Fried has been sentenced to 25 years in prison after being convicted on multiple counts of fraud and conspiracy related to the company's collapse.

- **Binance**: Binance, one of the world's largest cryptocurrency exchanges, has encountered regulatory challenges in several countries. Authorities in the U.S., U.K., Japan, and other nations have scrutinized Binance for its AML practices, leading to increased regulatory pressure. This has resulted in bans, warnings, and ongoing investigations, forcing Binance to enhance its compliance measures significantly. Despite these challenges, Binance continues to operate while bolstering its compliance team to meet regulatory standards and maintain its position in the market.

Future Regulatory Trends

As the cryptocurrency and blockchain industries continue to evolve, so too will the regulatory landscape. Future regulatory trends are likely to focus on balancing innovation with consumer protection and financial stability.

Central Bank Digital Currencies (CBDCs): One potential trend is the development of Central Bank Digital Currencies (CBDCs). Many countries are exploring or piloting CBDCs as a way to modernize their financial systems and provide a digital alternative to traditional cash. The introduction of CBDCs could lead to new regulatory frameworks governing their issuance, use, and interaction with existing cryptocurrencies. Countries like China, with its Digital Yuan, are leading the way in this area.

Environmental Sustainability: Environmental sustainability is becoming increasingly important. As concerns about the environmental impact of cryptocurrency mining grow, regulators may introduce measures to promote greener mining practices and the use of renewable energy sources. This trend is evident in the shift towards Proof of Stake (PoS) consensus mechanisms, which are more energy-efficient than traditional Proof of Work (PoW) systems.

Global Coordination and Harmonization: Global coordination and harmonization of regulations are also likely to become more prevalent. As cryptocurrencies and blockchain technology transcend national borders, international cooperation will be essential to address regulatory arbitrage and ensure a consistent regulatory approach. Organizations like the Financial

Action Task Force (FATF) are working to create global standards for cryptocurrency regulation.

Decentralized Finance (DeFi): The rise of Decentralized Finance (DeFi) presents unique regulatory challenges. DeFi platforms operate without intermediaries, making it difficult for regulators to enforce traditional compliance measures. Future regulations may need to adapt to address the risks and opportunities presented by DeFi, including the need for robust security measures and consumer protection.

Data Privacy and Security: As the use of blockchain technology expands, data privacy and security will become critical regulatory issues. Governments are likely to implement regulations to ensure that personal data is protected on blockchain networks, aligning with broader data protection laws such as the General Data Protection Regulation (GDPR) in the European Union.

Consumer Protection: Consumer protection will continue to be a focus of regulatory efforts. Ensuring that consumers are protected from fraud, scams, and financial losses is essential for fostering trust in the cryptocurrency market. Regulations may include requirements for transparency, disclosure of risks, and mechanisms for dispute resolution.

Innovation and Regulatory Sandboxes: To balance regulation and innovation, some countries are adopting regulatory sandboxes. These are controlled environments where blockchain and cryptocurrency projects can operate with regulatory oversight but without the full regulatory burden. This approach allows regulators to monitor developments and understand new technologies while allowing innovators to test their solutions.

Impact on Innovation

Regulation and compliance play a crucial role in shaping the innovation landscape in the cryptocurrency and blockchain industries. Clear and supportive regulatory frameworks can foster innovation by providing legal certainty and protecting investors. Conversely, overly restrictive regulations can stifle innovation and drive businesses to more favorable jurisdictions.

Attracting Investment and Talent: Regulatory clarity can attract investment and talent to the industry, as businesses and individuals are more likely to engage in activities that are well-regulated and legally compliant. Countries with supportive regulatory environments, such as Switzerland and Malta, have become hubs for blockchain and cryptocurrency innovation.

Cost of Compliance: However, compliance with regulations can be costly and time-consuming. Small businesses and startups may struggle to navigate complex regulatory requirements, potentially hindering their growth and innovation. Policymakers must strike a balance between protecting consumers and fostering an environment conducive to innovation.

Technological Advancements: Regulations can also drive technological advancements. For example, the need for compliance with AML and KYC regulations has led to the development of innovative identity verification and anti-fraud solutions. Similarly, environmental regulations can spur the adoption of more sustainable mining practices and energy-efficient blockchain technologies.

Global Competition: Countries compete to attract blockchain and cryptocurrency businesses by creating favorable regulatory environments. This competition can lead to a race to the top, with countries striving to provide the most innovative and supportive regulatory frameworks to attract businesses and talent.

Collaboration and Standards: Collaboration between regulators, industry participants, and international organizations is essential for developing effective regulatory standards. Such collaboration can help create a harmonized approach to regulation, reducing regulatory fragmentation and fostering a more stable and predictable environment for innovation.

Summary

The regulatory and compliance landscape for cryptocurrencies and blockchain technology is complex and varies significantly across different jurisdictions. Understanding global regulatory frameworks, navigating legal challenges, and staying informed about future regulatory trends are crucial for anyone involved in this space. While supportive regulations can foster innovation and attract investment, overly restrictive measures can stifle growth and drive businesses to more favorable jurisdictions. Balancing consumer protection, financial stability, and innovation is essential for shaping the future of the cryptocurrency and blockchain industries.

QUOTE

> *"Regulation and innovation can go hand in hand if done thoughtfully. The goal is to create a framework that fosters growth while protecting consumers and the financial system."*
>
> – Hester Peirce, SEC Commissioner

DEFINITIONS

1. **Securities and Exchange Commission (SEC)**: A U.S. government agency responsible for regulating the securities markets, ensuring investor protection, fair markets, and capital formation.

2. **Commodity Futures Trading Commission (CFTC)**: A U.S. government agency that regulates the derivatives markets, including futures, swaps, and certain types of options.

3. **Financial Crimes Enforcement Network (FinCEN)**: A bureau of the U.S. Department of the Treasury that combats money laundering, terrorism financing, and other financial crimes.

4. **Markets in Crypto-Assets (MiCA)**: A proposed regulatory framework by the European Union aiming to create a unified legal framework for cryptocurrencies.

5. **Financial Services Agency (FSA)**: Japan's regulatory body that oversees the financial sector, including cryptocurrency exchanges.

6. **Central Bank Digital Currency (CBDC)**: A digital form of central bank-issued currency designed to modernize financial systems and provide a digital alternative to traditional cash.

7. **Monetary Authority of Singapore (MAS)**: Singapore's central bank and financial regulatory authority.

8. **Howey Test**: A legal test used by the SEC to determine whether a cryptocurrency is considered a security, based on investment contracts and expectations of profit from the efforts of others.

QUIZ

Regulation and Compliance

1. **What role does the SEC play in the cryptocurrency market?**

   a) It regulates banks and insurance companies exclusively.

   b) It applies the Howey Test to determine if a cryptocurrency is a security and enforces securities laws for transparency and legality.

   c) It issues digital currencies for the U.S. government.

   d) It manages crypto taxation directly.

2. **How does the CFTC's regulation impact the cryptocurrency market?**

   a) It sets interest rates for cryptocurrencies.

   b) It regulates U.S. derivatives markets, including futures contracts based on cryptocurrencies.

   c) It oversees central bank digital currencies.

   d) It monitors NFTs and DeFi platforms exclusively.

3. **What are the primary functions of FinCEN in relation to cryptocurrencies?**

   a) Regulating stock exchanges.

   b) Promoting cryptocurrency mining.

   c) Combating money laundering and enforcing AML/KYC compliance among crypto businesses.

   d) Developing new cryptocurrencies.

4. **What is MiCA, and how does it affect the European cryptocurrency market?**

    a) A framework to unify EU crypto regulations and protect investors while fostering innovation.

    b) A blockchain project developing decentralized apps.

    c) A private cryptocurrency exchange based in Germany.

    d) A regulation banning all crypto activity in the EU.

5. **Describe the role of Japan's FSA in the cryptocurrency industry.**

    a) Issuing NFTs through Japanese banks.

    b) Overseeing cryptocurrency exchanges by enforcing AML and consumer protection measures.

    c) Launching the Digital Yen for everyday transactions.

    d) Managing global crypto mining operations.

6. **What is a CBDC? Provide an example of a country exploring its use.**

    a) A cryptocurrency created by private companies; the U.S. Dollar.

    b) A decentralized stablecoin with no government control; El Salvador.

    c) A digital form of government-issued currency; China's Digital Yuan.

    d) An investment token for blockchain startups; Japan's crypto ETF.

7. **How does the Monetary Authority of Singapore (MAS) support the cryptocurrency market?**

    a) By banning all forms of crypto trading.

    b) By providing clear guidelines for exchanges and requiring compliance with AML/KYC standards.

    c) By creating government-owned mining farms.

    d) By regulating traditional banks' interest rates on crypto loans.

8. **Why is the Howey Test significant in the context of cryptocurrency regulation?**

a) It determines if a cryptocurrency should be classified as property for tax purposes.

b) It identifies when a cryptocurrency should be regulated as a security by the SEC.

c) It sets energy consumption standards for crypto mining.

d) It classifies NFTs as securities automatically.

☑ ANSWER KEY WITH DETAILED EXPLANATIONS

1. b) It applies the Howey Test to determine if a cryptocurrency is a security and enforces securities laws for transparency and legality.

   Explanation:

   The SEC ensures investor protection by regulating securities markets, applying the Howey Test to cryptocurrencies, and enforcing disclosure and registration requirements when necessary.

2. b) It regulates U.S. derivatives markets, including futures contracts based on cryptocurrencies.

   Explanation:

   The CFTC oversees futures and derivatives, including Bitcoin and Ethereum futures, ensuring that trading is conducted fairly and transparently.

3. c) Combating money laundering and enforcing AML/KYC compliance among crypto businesses.

   Explanation:

   FinCEN enforces anti-money laundering laws, requiring crypto businesses to verify users' identities and monitor transactions for suspicious activity.

4. a) A framework to unify EU crypto regulations and protect investors while fostering innovation.

   Explanation:

   MiCA aims to create a consistent and harmonized crypto regulatory environment across EU member states, boosting clarity and encouraging blockchain innovation.

5. **b) Overseeing cryptocurrency exchanges by enforcing AML and consumer protection measures.**

    Explanation:

    Japan's FSA enforces strict regulatory standards for crypto exchanges to ensure security, transparency, and consumer trust.

6. **c) A digital form of government-issued currency; China's Digital Yuan.**

    Explanation:

    CBDCs, like China's Digital Yuan, represent modernized government-backed money designed to streamline payments and offer a secure digital cash alternative.

7. **b) By providing clear guidelines for exchanges and requiring compliance with AML/KYC standards.**

    Explanation:

    Singapore's MAS fosters a safe and innovative crypto environment by requiring exchanges to follow strong AML/KYC practices and providing transparent regulatory frameworks.

8. b) It identifies when a cryptocurrency should be regulated as a security by the SEC.

    Explanation:

    The Howey Test is crucial because it determines whether cryptocurrencies must comply with securities laws based on whether users invest money expecting profits derived from others' efforts.

CHAPTER 9

CHALLENGES AND OPPORTUNITIES

Key Points

- Security Concerns and Solutions
- Scalability Issues
- Future Trends and Innovations
- Overcoming Technological Barriers

CONTENT

Security Concerns and Solutions

Security is a paramount concern in the cryptocurrency and blockchain space. The decentralized nature of these technologies offers enhanced security features, but it also introduces unique challenges.

Hacks and Cyber Attacks Cryptocurrencies and blockchain networks have been targets of various cyber attacks, including hacking, phishing, and malware. High-profile incidents, such as the Mt. Gox exchange hack in 2014 and the more recent attacks on decentralized finance (DeFi) platforms, have resulted in significant financial losses. These incidents highlight the vulnerabilities within the ecosystem and the need for robust security measures.

Cold Storage and Hardware Wallets One of the most effective ways to secure cryptocurrencies is through cold storage, which involves keeping private keys offline and away from potential cyber threats. Hardware wallets, such as Ledger and Trezor, are popular cold storage solutions that provide a secure way to store private keys offline while still allowing users to access their funds when needed.

Multi-Signature Wallets Multi-signature (multi-sig) wallets require multiple private keys to authorize a transaction. This adds an extra layer of security by ensuring that no single individual can access the funds without the approval of other key holders. Multi-sig wallets are commonly used by businesses and organizations to safeguard their assets and prevent unauthorized access.

Regular Audits and Penetration Testing Conducting regular security audits and employing ethical hackers to perform penetration testing can help identify and address vulnerabilities in blockchain networks and applications. These proactive measures are essential for maintaining the integrity and security of the ecosystem.

Regulatory Compliance and Best Practices Adhering to regulatory compliance and implementing industry best practices, such as Know Your Customer (KYC) and Anti-Money Laundering (AML) protocols, can enhance the security of cryptocurrency exchanges and wallets. These measures help prevent illicit activities and ensure that platforms operate within legal frameworks.

Scalability Issues

Scalability is one of the most significant challenges facing blockchain technology. As the number of users and transactions increases, blockchain networks can experience congestion, leading to slower transaction times and higher fees.

Proof of Work (PoW) and Proof of Stake (PoS) The scalability issues of blockchain networks are often linked to their consensus mechanisms. Proof of Work (PoW), used by Bitcoin, is secure but resource-intensive and slow. Proof of Stake (PoS), used by Ethereum 2.0, aims to improve scalability by reducing the need for extensive computational power. PoS achieves consensus through validators who lock up a portion of their cryptocurrency as collateral.

Layer 2 Solutions Layer 2 solutions, such as the Lightning Network for Bitcoin and Plasma for Ethereum, aim to improve scalability by processing transactions off the main blockchain. These solutions can handle thousands of transactions per second, significantly reducing congestion on the main network and lowering transaction costs.

Sharding Sharding is another approach to improving blockchain scalability. It involves dividing the blockchain into smaller, more manageable pieces called shards, each capable of processing transactions independently. This parallel processing increases the overall throughput of the network, allowing it to handle more transactions simultaneously.

Blockchain Interoperability Interoperability between different blockchain networks can also enhance scalability. Projects like Polkadot and Cosmos are developing protocols that enable multiple blockchains to communicate and share information seamlessly. This interconnectedness allows for more efficient use of resources and reduces the strain on individual networks.

Future Trends and Innovations

The cryptocurrency and blockchain landscape is ever-changing, with constant advancements and innovations poised to significantly impact the future of the industry. Emerging trends such as Decentralized Finance (DeFi) and Non-Fungible Tokens (NFTs) are transforming traditional financial systems and the digital art market. Additionally, Central Bank Digital Currencies (CBDCs) are being explored by central banks globally, aiming to merge the benefits of cryptocurrencies with the stability of fiat currencies. Enterprise blockchain solutions are gaining traction across various sectors, enhancing transparency, security, and efficiency in business operations. Moreover, environmental sustainability is becoming a focal point, with efforts to mitigate the ecological footprint of blockchain technologies, particularly those reliant on Proof of Work (PoW). As these trends continue to evolve, they promise to redefine the boundaries and capabilities of blockchain and cryptocurrency technologies.

Decentralized Finance (DeFi)

DeFi has gained significant traction in the cryptocurrency space, offering a range of financial services without traditional intermediaries such as banks and brokers. DeFi platforms leverage smart contracts to automate processes, providing greater transparency and accessibility. These platforms enable users to lend, borrow, trade, and earn interest on their digital assets.

One of the key benefits of DeFi is financial inclusion. By eliminating the need for a central authority, DeFi opens up financial services to anyone with an internet connection and a digital wallet. This democratization of finance can empower individuals in regions with limited access to traditional banking services. Additionally, DeFi platforms are often more efficient and cost-effective, reducing fees and transaction times compared to conventional financial systems.

The growth of DeFi has also spurred innovation in financial products. Yield farming, for example, allows users to earn rewards by providing liquidity to DeFi protocols. Decentralized exchanges (DEXs) like Uniswap and SushiSwap enable peer-to-peer trading of cryptocurrencies without the need for a central exchange, enhancing security and privacy for users.

However, DeFi is not without its challenges. The reliance on smart contracts introduces technical risks, as vulnerabilities in the code can lead to significant financial losses. Furthermore, the regulatory environment for DeFi is still evolving, and future regulations could impact the growth and operation of DeFi platforms.

Non-Fungible Tokens (NFTs)

NFTs have exploded in popularity, transforming the way we think about digital ownership. Unlike cryptocurrencies, which are fungible and can be exchanged on a one-to-one basis, NFTs are unique digital assets that represent ownership of a specific item, such as digital art, music, videos, and even virtual real estate. Each NFT is stored on a blockchain, ensuring its uniqueness and provenance.

NFTs provide creators with new ways to monetize their work. Artists, musicians, and other creators can sell their digital creations directly to consumers without intermediaries, earning royalties on subsequent sales. This has opened up new revenue streams and markets, particularly in the arts and entertainment industries. For example, platforms like OpenSea and Rarible allow creators to mint, sell, and trade NFTs, reaching a global audience.

The popularity of NFTs has also led to the development of virtual worlds and metaverses, where users can buy, sell, and trade virtual goods and real estate. Projects like Decentraland and The Sandbox are pioneering this space, creating immersive environments where NFTs play a central role in the economy.

Despite their potential, NFTs also face criticism and challenges. The environmental impact of minting and trading NFTs on PoW blockchains like Ethereum has raised concerns. Additionally, the speculative nature of the NFT market can lead to volatility and the risk of bubbles. Ensuring the authenticity and value of NFTs also remains a challenge, with instances of plagiarism and fraud reported.

Central Bank Digital Currencies (CBDCs)

Central banks worldwide are exploring the development of CBDCs, digital versions of fiat currencies. CBDCs aim to combine the benefits of cryptocurrencies, such as fast and secure transactions, with the stability and trust associated with traditional currencies. The implementation of CBDCs could revolutionize the global financial system, providing a modern, digital alternative to physical cash.

One of the primary goals of CBDCs is to enhance the efficiency and security of payment systems. CBDCs can facilitate faster and cheaper cross-border transactions, reduce the reliance on cash, and improve financial inclusion by providing access to digital financial services for unbanked populations. Additionally, CBDCs can provide central banks with better tools for monitoring and controlling the money supply, enhancing monetary policy effectiveness.

Countries like China, Sweden, and the Bahamas are at the forefront of CBDC development. China's Digital Yuan pilot program has been extensively tested in various cities, with millions of users participating. Sweden's e-Krona project aims to ensure the country's payment systems remain robust and accessible in a digital economy. The Bahamas' Sand Dollar is one of the first fully operational CBDCs, providing a model for other countries to follow.

However, the adoption of CBDCs also presents challenges. Ensuring privacy and security while preventing illicit activities is a critical concern. The design of CBDCs must balance the need for user anonymity with regulatory requirements for AML and KYC compliance. Additionally, the impact of CBDCs on commercial banks and the financial stability of the existing banking system needs careful consideration.

Enterprise Blockchain Solutions

Beyond cryptocurrencies, blockchain technology is being adopted by enterprises for various use cases, including supply chain management, healthcare, and identity verification. These solutions leverage blockchain's transparency, security, and immutability to improve efficiency and trust in business processes.

In supply chain management, blockchain enhances transparency and traceability, enabling companies to track the movement of goods from origin to destination. This helps prevent fraud, ensure product authenticity, and improve efficiency. IBM's Food Trust blockchain, used by companies like Walmart and Nestlé, is a notable example of blockchain's impact on supply chains.

In healthcare, blockchain can secure patient records, ensuring data privacy and interoperability. Blockchain-based systems allow for seamless and secure sharing of medical information among healthcare providers, improving patient care and reducing administrative costs. The Estonian government's use of blockchain for securing health records is a pioneering example.

Identity verification is another area where blockchain is making a significant impact. Blockchain-based digital identities can provide secure and verifiable credentials for individuals and organizations. This can streamline processes such as KYC checks, reduce fraud, and enhance privacy. Projects like Microsoft's ION and the Sovrin Network are leading the way in decentralized identity solutions.

Despite the promise of enterprise blockchain solutions, challenges remain. Integrating blockchain with existing systems, achieving industry-wide standards, and ensuring data accuracy require significant effort and collaboration. Additionally, the regulatory landscape for blockchain applications is still evolving, necessitating ongoing dialogue between stakeholders and regulators.

Environmental Sustainability

The environmental impact of blockchain, particularly PoW-based networks like Bitcoin, has been a growing concern. PoW requires significant computational power, leading to high energy consumption and carbon emissions. As the demand for blockchain applications increases, addressing their environmental impact becomes crucial for the long-term viability of the technology.

One of the primary solutions to reduce the carbon footprint of blockchain is transitioning from PoW to PoS. PoS is more energy-efficient because it selects validators based on the number of coins they hold and are willing to "stake" as collateral, reducing the need for extensive computational power.

Ethereum's planned transition to PoS with Ethereum 2.0 is a significant step towards sustainability.

Another approach is using renewable energy sources for blockchain operations. Mining farms and data centers can be powered by solar, wind, or hydroelectric energy, reducing their reliance on fossil fuels. Some companies are already exploring these options to make their operations more sustainable.

Innovations in blockchain protocols also contribute to sustainability. Layer 2 solutions, such as the Lightning Network for Bitcoin and Optimistic Rollups for Ethereum, help increase transaction throughput and reduce the energy consumption of the main blockchain network. These solutions process transactions off-chain and only settle the final results on the main chain, making the system more efficient.

Additionally, blockchain can be used to promote environmental sustainability beyond its own ecosystem. Projects like Power Ledger and WePower use blockchain to enable peer-to-peer energy trading and support the transition to renewable energy sources. These projects demonstrate how blockchain can contribute to a more sustainable future.

Overall, sustainable blockchain practices are essential for the technology's long-term viability. Balancing the benefits of blockchain with its environmental impact requires ongoing innovation and collaboration among stakeholders to develop and implement greener solutions.

Overcoming Technological Barriers

While blockchain technology holds immense potential, several technological barriers must be overcome to realize its full benefits.

Energy Consumption The high energy consumption of PoW-based blockchains has raised environmental concerns. Transitioning to more energy-efficient consensus mechanisms, such as PoS, and integrating renewable energy sources are critical steps toward addressing these issues.

Usability and User Experience Improving the usability and user experience of blockchain applications is essential for widespread adoption. Simplifying the process of managing private keys, enhancing wallet interfaces, and providing user-friendly platforms can help attract a broader audience.

Regulatory Clarity Clear and consistent regulatory frameworks are necessary for the growth and stability of the cryptocurrency and blockchain industry. Policymakers must collaborate with industry stakeholders to develop regulations that protect consumers while fostering innovation.

Education and Awareness Educating the public about blockchain technology and its potential benefits is crucial for its adoption. Increasing awareness through educational programs, workshops, and accessible resources can help demystify the technology and encourage more people to participate in the ecosystem.

Interoperability Standards Developing interoperability standards that allow different blockchain networks to communicate and work together seamlessly is vital for the technology's future. Standardization efforts can help create a more connected and efficient blockchain ecosystem.

SUMMARY

The cryptocurrency and blockchain industry faces several challenges, including security concerns, scalability issues, and regulatory uncertainties. However, these challenges also present opportunities for innovation and growth. By addressing security vulnerabilities, improving scalability, and fostering regulatory clarity, the industry can overcome these barriers and unlock the full potential of blockchain technology. Future trends, such as DeFi, NFTs, CBDCs, and enterprise blockchain solutions, promise to drive the industry's evolution, offering new possibilities for financial inclusion, efficiency, and sustainability.

QUOTE

"The challenges facing blockchain and cryptocurrency today are not insurmountable. With innovation, collaboration, and regulatory clarity, we can unlock the full potential of this transformative technology."

– Vitalik Buterin, Co-founder of Ethereum

DEFINITIONS

1. **Cold Storage:** A method of storing cryptocurrencies offline to protect them from online hacks.
2. **Hardware Wallet:** A physical device that securely stores private keys offline.
3. **Multi-Signature Wallet:** A wallet that requires multiple private keys to authorize a transaction, adding an extra layer of security.

4. **Proof of Work (PoW):** A consensus mechanism that requires participants to solve complex mathematical problems to validate transactions and secure the network.

5. **Proof of Stake (PoS):** A consensus mechanism where validators are chosen to create new blocks and validate transactions based on the number of coins they hold and are willing to "stake" as collateral.

6. **Layer 2 Solutions:** Off-chain solutions that improve the scalability of blockchain networks by processing transactions outside the main blockchain.

7. **Sharding:** A scalability technique that involves dividing a blockchain into smaller, more manageable pieces called shards, each capable of processing transactions independently.

8. **Interoperability:** The ability of different blockchain networks to communicate and work together seamlessly.

9. **Non-Fungible Token (NFT):** A unique digital asset that represents ownership of a specific item, such as digital art or collectibles, and is stored on a blockchain.

10. **Central Bank Digital Currency (CBDC):** A digital form of central bank-issued currency designed to modernize financial systems and provide a digital alternative to traditional cash.

QUIZ

Challenges and Opportunities

1. **What is cold storage, and why is it important for cryptocurrency security?**

   a) A method of transferring cryptocurrencies to online exchanges quickly

   b) A way to protect cryptocurrencies by storing private keys offline, away from hackers

   c) A technique for increasing transaction speed

   d) A government-regulated database for crypto users

2. **How do hardware wallets protect private keys from online threats?**

   a) By storing keys in online cloud servers

   b) By encrypting public blockchains

   c) By keeping private keys offline in secure physical devices

   d) By automatically sending keys to multiple users

3. **What is the primary benefit of using multi-signature wallets?**

   a) Faster transaction speed

   b) Lower transaction fees

   c) Requiring multiple private keys to authorize a transaction, increasing security

   d) Enabling anonymous cryptocurrency trades

4. **How does Proof of Work (PoW) differ from Proof of Stake (PoS) in terms of energy consumption?**

a) PoW uses far less energy than PoS

b) PoW is more energy-efficient due to mining pools

c) PoW consumes more energy because it requires significant computational work, while PoS is energy-efficient by selecting validators

d) PoS wastes energy through transaction duplication

5. **What are Layer 2 solutions, and how do they improve blockchain scalability?**

a) Systems designed to create new cryptocurrencies

b) Off-chain protocols that process transactions faster and cheaper outside the main blockchain

c) Mining pools that combine resources to improve speed

d) Centralized servers built on top of blockchains

6. **How does sharding enhance the scalability of blockchain networks?**

a) By freezing inactive accounts

b) By breaking down blockchains into smaller pieces that process transactions independently

c) By copying blockchains across servers

d) By reducing the number of miners

7. **Why is interoperability important for the future of blockchain technology?**

a) It eliminates all mining activities

b) It allows different blockchain networks to communicate and share information seamlessly

c) It restricts data transfers between blockchains

d) It increases the price of tokens

8. **What are Non-Fungible Tokens (NFTs), and what are their primary use cases?**

   a) Regular cryptocurrencies like Bitcoin

   b) Unique digital assets that represent ownership of items like art, music, and virtual real estate

   c) Digital currencies used exclusively for gaming

   d) Anonymous tokens for cross-border payments

9. **How can Central Bank Digital Currencies (CBDCs) revolutionize the global financial system?**

   a) By eliminating all fiat currencies

   b) By replacing Bitcoin

   c) By providing fast, secure digital transactions backed by central banks

   d) By creating unregulated financial networks

10. **What role does regulatory clarity play in the growth and stability of the cryptocurrency and blockchain industry?**

   a) It creates more confusion about blockchain projects

   b) It provides a clear legal framework that encourages innovation and protects consumers

   c) It forces all cryptocurrencies to shut down

   d) It bans peer-to-peer trading

☑ ANSWER KEY WITH DETAILED EXPLANATIONS

1. **b) A way to protect cryptocurrencies by storing private keys offline, away from hackers**

   Explanation:

   Cold storage keeps private keys disconnected from the internet, dramatically reducing the risk of hacking or malware attacks on digital assets.

2. **c) By keeping private keys offline in secure physical devices**

   Explanation:

   Hardware wallets like Ledger and Trezor safeguard private keys by storing them offline, ensuring they are inaccessible to online threats.

3. **c) Requiring multiple private keys to authorize a transaction, increasing security**

   Explanation:

   Multi-signature wallets prevent unauthorized access by requiring two or more parties to approve a transaction, adding a layer of protection.

4. **c) PoW consumes more energy because it requires significant computational work, while PoS is energy-efficient by selecting validators**

   Explanation:

   PoW blockchains like Bitcoin use extensive computational resources for mining, whereas PoS blockchains like Ethereum 2.0 are more sustainable by choosing validators based on the cryptocurrency they stake.

5. b) Off-chain protocols that process transactions faster and cheaper outside the main blockchain

    Explanation:

    Layer 2 solutions, such as the Lightning Network, reduce congestion on main blockchains by moving transactions off-chain while ensuring they remain secure.

6. b) By breaking down blockchains into smaller pieces that process transactions independently

    Explanation:

    Sharding splits the blockchain into smaller units, allowing multiple parts to process transactions simultaneously, improving overall throughput and efficiency.

7. b) It allows different blockchain networks to communicate and share information seamlessly

    Explanation:

    Blockchain interoperability fosters cooperation between blockchains, enabling assets and information to move freely across different networks and enhancing innovation.

8. b) Unique digital assets that represent ownership of items like art, music, and virtual real estate

    Explanation:

    NFTs represent ownership rights to unique digital items, and their popularity spans across industries like art, music, collectibles, and gaming.

9. **c) By providing fast, secure digital transactions backed by central banks**

   Explanation:

   CBDCs combine the security and efficiency of blockchain with the trust and stability of government-backed currencies, modernizing the payment landscape.

10. **b) It provides a clear legal framework that encourages innovation and protects consumers**

    Explanation:

    Regulatory clarity reduces uncertainty, promotes trust, and allows businesses and investors to operate with confidence within the crypto and blockchain space.

CRYPTO AND BLOCKCHAIN ADOPTION: A GLOBAL PERSPECTIVE

Key Points

- Current Adoption Rates
- Barriers to Widespread Adoption
- Case Studies from Different Regions
- Strategies for Increasing Adoption

CONTENT

Current Adoption Rates

In 2023, approximately 420 million people globally owned or used cryptocurrencies, representing about 5.5% of the world's population. Just two years later, as of June 2025, that number has more than doubled—approximately 861 million people now engage with cryptocurrencies, accounting for over 10% of the global population.

Looking ahead, if current adoption trends continue, the next decade could bring even more widespread integration of digital assets into everyday life. By 2035, global cryptocurrency users could number between 2.5 to 3.5 billion, potentially representing 25% to 40% of the world's population. Driving this growth will be continued innovation in blockchain applications, increasing use of crypto for payments and financial services, expanding mobile access in emerging markets, tokenized assets, and rising adoption of decentralized systems by both individuals and institutions.

In countries like **Vietnam** and **Ukraine**, the use of cryptocurrency is becoming increasingly common, particularly among individuals seeking financial alternatives to unstable national currencies. The growth in decentralized finance (DeFi) services, peer-to-peer transactions, and cross-border payments has contributed significantly to the rise in cryptocurrency use in these countries.

In more developed economies such as the **United States**, **Germany**, and **Japan**, crypto adoption is being driven by institutional investments, such as hedge funds and publicly traded companies like **Tesla** and **MicroStrategy**, which have invested substantial amounts into Bitcoin and other cryptocurrencies. Additionally, financial services firms like **PayPal** and **Visa** have begun integrating crypto into their platforms, allowing everyday users to buy, hold, and use cryptocurrencies more seamlessly.

Barriers to Widespread Adoption

While cryptocurrency adoption is growing, there are several barriers that prevent wider mainstream acceptance:

1. **Regulatory Uncertainty**: One of the biggest hurdles to cryptocurrency adoption is the lack of clear regulations in many regions. Countries like **China** and **India** have implemented strict regulations

or outright bans on cryptocurrency trading and mining activities, creating uncertainty for businesses and individuals. In contrast, nations like the **United States** have a more ambiguous stance, where the regulatory environment is evolving but still lacks uniformity.

2. **Volatility**: Cryptocurrencies, particularly **Bitcoin** and **Ethereum**, have been known for their price volatility. This instability discourages many potential users from adopting digital currencies for daily transactions, as the value can fluctuate drastically within short periods.

3. **Technological Barriers**: Scalability issues continue to plague popular blockchain networks like **Bitcoin** and **Ethereum**, where transaction times and fees increase during periods of high demand. Although second-layer solutions such as the **Lightning Network** for Bitcoin and **Ethereum's Layer 2** rollups are helping to address these issues, the technology is still in its infancy and requires further development for mass adoption.

4. **Public Perception and Misinformation**: Many individuals are still unaware or misinformed about how cryptocurrencies work. A lack of trust, stemming from high-profile hacks (e.g., **Mt. Gox**) and scams, has created a negative image in some circles. Moreover, many consumers do not fully understand blockchain technology and view it as complex or risky.

Case Studies from Different Regions

1. **El Salvador**: In 2021, El Salvador became the first country to adopt **Bitcoin** as legal tender, with President Nayib Bukele leading the charge. The goal was to reduce the cost of remittances (a major source of income for many Salvadorans) and foster financial

inclusion. However, despite the ambitious goals, the adoption has been met with mixed results. The **Chivo Wallet**, a government-issued digital wallet, saw initial downloads spike, but reports indicate low sustained usage due to concerns about Bitcoin's volatility and technical difficulties with the wallet.

2. **Nigeria**: The adoption of cryptocurrencies in Nigeria has surged due to factors such as the devaluation of the Nigerian naira and inflation. Nigerians use cryptocurrencies for international remittances and as a hedge against inflation. Despite regulatory crackdowns from the **Central Bank of Nigeria** banning banks from servicing crypto companies, peer-to-peer trading volumes have skyrocketed, making Nigeria one of the largest markets for Bitcoin in the world.

3. **Switzerland**: Switzerland's **Crypto Valley** in Zug is a global hub for blockchain and cryptocurrency companies. The country's supportive regulatory framework, transparent tax policies, and progressive stance toward digital assets have attracted a large number of startups and institutional investors. The **Swiss Financial Market Supervisory Authority (FINMA)** has provided clear guidelines for Initial Coin Offerings (ICOs), crypto exchanges, and DeFi projects, making Switzerland a haven for blockchain innovation.

4. **Japan**: Japan has been one of the most forward-thinking nations regarding cryptocurrency regulations. After the infamous **Mt. Gox** hack, Japan introduced strict regulations for cryptocurrency exchanges, requiring them to register with the **Financial Services Agency (FSA)**. This proactive approach has made Japan a leading market for digital currencies, with widespread adoption in both retail and institutional sectors.

Strategies for Increasing Adoption

1. **Regulatory Clarity**: For cryptocurrency adoption to grow, it's crucial that governments and regulatory bodies provide clear and consistent guidelines for the industry. The creation of **regulatory sandboxes**, such as those in **Singapore** and the **UK**, allows businesses to innovate while remaining compliant with evolving regulations.

2. **Institutional Involvement**: The increasing adoption of cryptocurrencies by large corporations, such as **Tesla**, **PayPal**, and **Visa**, has significantly legitimized the crypto space. As more companies begin accepting or holding crypto, consumer confidence is likely to grow. Additionally, institutional investment in the crypto sector, from hedge funds and asset managers, has provided much-needed liquidity to the market.

3. **Financial Inclusion**: Many of the unbanked populations in regions like **Africa** and **Southeast Asia** are driving the adoption of cryptocurrencies as they provide easier access to financial services without needing traditional bank accounts. Enhancing mobile access and providing educational programs for these populations can significantly increase global crypto adoption rates.

4. **Education and Awareness**: To demystify cryptocurrencies and foster trust, there needs to be widespread educational initiatives that help users understand the benefits and risks of using digital currencies. Governments, private organizations, and academic institutions can collaborate to offer blockchain and crypto literacy programs to the general public.

5. **Technological Improvements**: Increasing blockchain scalability and improving user interfaces can help more individuals adopt crypto for everyday use. **Ethereum 2.0**, **Cardano**, and **Polkadot** are

all working on solutions to reduce transaction fees, increase speed, and enhance security, making cryptocurrencies more practical for real-world applications.

SUMMARY

Chapter 10 provides a comprehensive look at the state of global cryptocurrency and blockchain adoption. It highlights both the significant strides that certain regions have made—like **El Salvador**, **Nigeria**, and **Switzerland**—and the barriers that still exist, such as regulatory uncertainty, technological challenges, and public skepticism.

By examining case studies from various regions, the chapter illustrates the diversity in adoption trends and the unique factors driving them. For example, while **Nigeria** adopts cryptocurrencies out of necessity to bypass inflation, **Switzerland** has built an ecosystem that encourages innovation through clear regulations.

The chapter also presents strategies for increasing adoption, emphasizing the importance of regulatory clarity, institutional involvement, financial inclusion, education, and technological advancements. As the global financial landscape evolves, cryptocurrencies are poised to play an increasingly important role in shaping the future.

QUOTE

"The adoption of digital currency is not just about technology. It's about reshaping the financial systems to make them more inclusive, transparent, and accessible for everyone."

— Vitalik Buterin, Co-Founder of Ethereum

DEFINITIONS

1. **Cryptocurrency Adoption Rate**: The percentage of individuals or businesses within a specific population who actively use or own cryptocurrencies.

2. **Regulatory Sandbox**: A framework set up by regulators that allows businesses to test innovative financial products and services within a controlled environment under regulatory oversight.

3. **Layer 2 Solutions**: Secondary frameworks or protocols built on top of a blockchain to improve its scalability, efficiency, and speed.

4. **DeFi (Decentralized Finance)**: A movement that uses blockchain technology to provide financial services without relying on traditional financial intermediaries like banks.

5. **Central Bank Digital Currency (CBDC)**: Digital money issued by a central bank, offering a stable and secure alternative to volatile cryptocurrencies.

6. **Peer-to-Peer (P2P) Transactions**: Direct transfers of assets or information between individuals without an intermediary.

7. **Institutional Adoption**: The process by which established financial institutions and large corporations integrate cryptocurrency into their operations.

8. **Scalability**: The capacity of a blockchain network to handle a growing number of transactions while maintaining speed and efficiency.

QUIZ

Crypto and Blockchain Adoption
– A Global Perspective

1. What country became the first to adopt Bitcoin as legal tender?

   a) Switzerland

   b) El Salvador

   c) Japan

   d) Nigeria

2. What is the biggest barrier to widespread crypto adoption?

   a) Public awareness

   b) Regulatory uncertainty

   c) Blockchain speed

   d) Transaction fees

3. How do regulatory sandboxes benefit blockchain startups?

   a) By reducing operational costs

   b) By allowing companies to test new technologies under regulatory oversight

   c) By attracting institutional investors

   d) By offering government subsidies

4. **What is a Layer 2 solution in blockchain technology?**

   a) A new cryptocurrency

   b) A secondary protocol designed to improve scalability and speed on a blockchain

   c) A tax benefit for cryptocurrency holders

   d) A regulatory framework for international transactions

5. **What are the benefits of Central Bank Digital Currencies (CBDCs)?**

   a) They eliminate the need for traditional banking

   b) They provide a stable digital alternative backed by central banks

   c) They replace fiat currencies entirely

   d) They are only used for international transactions

6. **What was one of the key reasons behind Nigeria's surge in cryptocurrency adoption?**

   a) Government endorsement

   b) High inflation and the devaluation of the naira

   c) Institutional interest from large banks

   d) Foreign investment in crypto startups

7. **What is a significant challenge for blockchain scalability?**

   a) Lack of institutional interest

   b) The volatility of cryptocurrency prices

   c) Increasing transaction times and fees during high demand

   d) Lack of developer interest

8. **How has Switzerland's regulatory environment contributed to its position as a blockchain hub?**

   a) Strict regulatory framework

   b) Clear guidelines for crypto and blockchain startups

   c) Minimal tax incentives

   d) Ban on cryptocurrency transactions

9. **How do financial literacy programs contribute to cryptocurrency adoption?**

   a) They encourage government regulation of cryptocurrencies

   b) They educate the public on the benefits and risks of using digital currencies

   c) They limit public interest in cryptocurrencies

   d) They reduce cryptocurrency prices

10. **What role does institutional involvement play in increasing crypto adoption?**

   a) It creates price stability

   b) It enhances the legitimacy of cryptocurrencies and integrates them into existing financial systems

   c) It reduces regulatory risks

   d) It decreases the need for blockchain developers

☑ ANSWER KEY WITH DETAILED EXPLANATIONS

1. b) El Salvador

    Explanation:

    El Salvador became the first country to adopt Bitcoin as legal tender in 2021 to lower remittance costs and boost financial inclusion, though adoption has seen mixed success.

2. b) Regulatory uncertainty

    Explanation:

    Without clear laws and regulations, businesses and individuals are hesitant to adopt cryptocurrencies, stalling growth and innovation.

3. b) By allowing companies to test new technologies under regulatory oversight

    Explanation:

    Regulatory sandboxes let blockchain startups innovate in a monitored environment, minimizing risks while fostering new ideas.

4. b) A secondary protocol designed to improve scalability and speed on a blockchain

    Explanation:

    Layer 2 solutions, like the Lightning Network and Ethereum rollups, help blockchains process transactions faster and at lower cost.

5. b) They provide a stable digital alternative backed by central banks

    Explanation:

    CBDCs offer the benefits of digital transactions while maintaining the stability and trust associated with government-backed currencies.

6. **b) High inflation and the devaluation of the naira**

   Explanation:

   Faced with economic instability, many Nigerians turned to Bitcoin and stablecoins to preserve the value of their money and facilitate cross-border transactions.

7. **c) Increasing transaction times and fees during high demand**

   Explanation:

   Scalability issues lead to network congestion, driving up transaction fees and slowing down processing times, making blockchains less practical for everyday use.

8. **b) Clear guidelines for crypto and blockchain startups**

   Explanation:

   Switzerland's proactive regulations made it a favorable environment for blockchain innovation, attracting startups and investors from around the world.

9. **b) They educate the public on the benefits and risks of using digital currencies**

   Explanation:

   Educational initiatives help build trust, demystify blockchain technology, and encourage responsible participation in the crypto economy.

10. **b) It enhances the legitimacy of cryptocurrencies and integrates them into existing financial systems**

    Explanation:

    Institutional adoption by firms like PayPal, Tesla, and Visa signals to the public and regulators that crypto is becoming a recognized part of the global economy.

CHAPTER 11

CRYPTO AND BLOCKCHAIN IN EDUCATION

Key Points

- Integrating Blockchain in Educational Institutions
- Blockchain Credentials and Certifications
- Educating the Next Generation of Crypto Enthusiasts
- Developing Blockchain Curriculums
- The Future of Blockchain in Education

CONTENT

Integrating Blockchain in Educational Institutions

Blockchain technology fundamentally changes how educational institutions manage, deliver, and verify academic content and credentials. The potential for blockchain to enhance efficiency, security, and transparency in education is vast, with numerous institutions worldwide beginning to explore its applications.

One of the most significant impacts of blockchain in education is the issuance of **Digital Credentials**. Traditionally, verifying academic qualifications has been a time-consuming process fraught with the risk of fraud. Blockchain allows institutions to issue tamper-proof digital credentials, ensuring that qualifications are easily verifiable by employers and other educational institutions. This is crucial in an era where online education is becoming more prevalent, and the need for secure, verifiable credentials is paramount.

For example, the Massachusetts Institute of Technology (MIT) has implemented a blockchain-based system for issuing digital diplomas. These digital credentials can be stored in a digital wallet and shared with potential employers, ensuring that the information is secure and tamper-proof. This system not only enhances the security of academic credentials but also simplifies the verification process for employers, making it easier to confirm the authenticity of a candidate's qualifications.

Another key application of blockchain in educational institutions is in **Automating Administrative Processes**. Administrative tasks such as student admissions, financial aid processing, and course registration can be complex and time-consuming. Blockchain technology can streamline these processes through the use of smart contracts. These are self-executing contracts where the terms of the agreement are directly written into code. Smart contracts can automatically verify and process applications, reducing the workload for administrative staff and minimizing errors. This can result in significant cost savings for institutions and make the administration of educational services more efficient.

The University of Nicosia in Cyprus is a leading example of how blockchain can increase efficiency and reduce operational costs in education. The university has integrated blockchain technology to manage its records and automate various administrative processes. This has not only improved efficiency but also enhanced the security and transparency of the university's operations.

Blockchain Credentials and Certifications

The issuance and verification of educational credentials are areas where blockchain technology is having a transformative impact. Traditional methods of issuing diplomas, certificates, and other qualifications are often slow, costly, and prone to fraud. Blockchain offers a more secure and efficient alternative.

Educational institutions can issue digital credentials on a blockchain, making them easily verifiable and tamper-proof. These credentials can be shared globally without the need for intermediaries, facilitating cross-border education and employment opportunities. This is particularly beneficial in an increasingly globalized world where students often study in one country and seek employment in another.

For example, MIT has started issuing digital diplomas using blockchain technology. These diplomas are stored on a blockchain, allowing graduates to easily share their credentials with potential employers or other institutions. This initiative showcases the potential of blockchain in revolutionizing the way educational credentials are managed and verified.

Blockchain credentials also offer greater accessibility. Students can have lifetime access to their academic records and certifications, which they can easily share with others whenever needed. This portability and accessibility make blockchain credentials particularly beneficial in today's digital age, where individuals often need to prove their qualifications across various platforms and contexts.

Moreover, blockchain can help combat the growing issue of credential fraud. By ensuring that all academic records and certifications are stored on a tamper-proof blockchain, educational institutions can significantly reduce the risk of fake credentials being issued or used.

Educating the Next Generation of Crypto Enthusiasts

As blockchain and cryptocurrency become increasingly relevant across various industries, there is a growing need to educate the next generation of crypto enthusiasts. Educational institutions are beginning to incorporate blockchain and cryptocurrency into their curricula, recognizing the importance of these technologies in the future of finance, technology, and beyond.

Comprehensive Blockchain Curricula are being developed to cover the fundamentals of blockchain technology, cryptocurrency, and decentralized applications (dApps). These programs aim to equip students with the knowledge and skills needed to thrive in the emerging blockchain industry. Universities such as Stanford and Berkeley are at the forefront of this movement, offering courses that delve into topics such as cryptography, consensus mechanisms, smart contracts, and the regulatory landscape.

Hands-on Training is also crucial in blockchain education. Students can participate in workshops, hackathons, and internships that provide practical experience in blockchain development and application. For example, the Blockchain at Berkeley student organization offers various hands-on activities, helping students understand the real-world applications of blockchain technology. This practical experience is invaluable in preparing students for careers in the blockchain industry.

Industry Partnerships are another essential component of blockchain education. By collaborating with leading companies in the blockchain space, educational institutions can provide students with valuable insights and opportunities to engage with real-world projects. These partnerships can also facilitate research and development in blockchain technology, driving innovation in the field.

Developing Blockchain Curriculums

The development of comprehensive blockchain curricula is essential for preparing students for careers in the rapidly evolving tech landscape. These programs should cover both the theoretical foundations and practical applications of blockchain technology, ensuring that students are well-prepared for the blockchain industry.

Theoretical foundations are a crucial part of any blockchain curriculum. Courses should cover the underlying principles of blockchain technology, including cryptography, distributed systems, and consensus mechanisms. Understanding these concepts is essential for grasping how blockchain works and its potential applications.

Practical applications are equally important. Students should learn about the real-world uses of blockchain technology in various industries, such as finance, healthcare, supply chain management, and voting systems. By exploring these applications, students can better understand how blockchain can be leveraged to solve real-world problems.

Project-based Learning is an effective way to integrate practical applications into the curriculum. Students can work on projects that involve developing and implementing blockchain-based solutions to real-world challenges.

This hands-on approach not only reinforces theoretical knowledge but also provides students with valuable experience in blockchain development.

One example of a comprehensive blockchain curriculum is the program offered by the University of Edinburgh, which covers both the theoretical and practical aspects of blockchain technology. This program includes courses on cryptography, distributed systems, and blockchain applications, as well as a project-based component where students can develop their blockchain solutions.

The Future of Blockchain in Education

As EdTech continues to evolve, blockchain is poised to play a central role in the future of education. From enhancing the security and transparency of academic records to creating new models of decentralized learning, blockchain technology offers numerous opportunities to improve the educational experience.

In addition to the practical applications already being explored, future innovations could include fully Decentralized Education Systems that operate entirely on blockchain, providing universal access to high-quality education. These systems could leverage smart contracts to manage all aspects of the educational process, from enrollment to assessment and certification, creating a more efficient and equitable education system.

Overall, the integration of blockchain into educational institutions is just beginning, but the potential impact on the way we manage, deliver, and verify education is vast. As blockchain technology continues to evolve, its role in the educational sector will likely expand, bringing about significant changes in how we approach learning and credentialing in the digital age.

SUMMARY

Blockchain technology is revolutionizing the education sector by introducing innovative ways to manage, verify, and deliver educational content. Integrating blockchain into educational institutions has led to more secure, efficient, and transparent processes. Institutions like MIT have implemented blockchain-based systems to issue digital diplomas, ensuring credentials are tamper-proof and easily verifiable.

Blockchain also enhances the issuance and verification of educational certifications, with smart contracts automating these processes, thus reducing fraud and administrative burdens. Online learning platforms are beginning to adopt blockchain for secure and transparent credentialing.

Moreover, as blockchain and cryptocurrency become more integral to various industries, there is a growing emphasis on educating the next generation of crypto enthusiasts. Universities are developing comprehensive blockchain curricula that cover both theoretical foundations and practical applications. These programs, supported by industry partnerships, equip students with the necessary knowledge and skills to excel in the blockchain space.

Looking ahead, blockchain's role in education is poised to grow, with the potential to transform how academic records are managed, how credentials are issued, and how learning is incentivized and tracked. This chapter explores these developments and highlights the transformative impact of blockchain on education.

QUOTE

"Blockchain will have the same transformative effect on education that the internet has had on business."

— Jeff Selingo, Author and Higher Education Expert

DEFINITIONS:

1. **Blockchain**: In the educational sector, a blockchain is a decentralized digital ledger used to securely record and verify academic records, certifications, and credentials. This ensures that student achievements are immutable and can be easily shared with employers or other institutions.

2. **Smart Contract**: A smart contract in education is a self-executing code within a blockchain that automatically enforces agreements related to academic activities, such as issuing diplomas or certificates when specific conditions, like course completion, are met.

3. **Digital Credentials**: Digital credentials refer to academic certifications and degrees that are issued and verified on a blockchain. These credentials are secure, easily accessible, and can be shared globally, providing a tamper-proof record of educational achievements.

4. **Cryptography**: Within the context of educational data, cryptography is the practice of encoding sensitive information, such as student records, to protect it from unauthorized access. This ensures the privacy and security of data stored on educational blockchains.

5. **Consensus Mechanism**: A consensus mechanism in educational blockchains is the process through which all participants in the network agree on the validity of academic records and transactions, ensuring that the data is accurate and trustworthy.

6. **Distributed Systems**: In education, distributed systems refer to the use of interconnected computers across multiple locations that work together to store and manage educational data on a block-chain, enhancing security and accessibility.

7. **Hackathon**: A hackathon in the educational context is an event where students and educators collaborate intensively to develop innovative blockchain-based educational tools and solutions, fostering hands-on learning and creativity.

8. **Decentralized Application (dApp)**: A decentralized application in education is a software tool built on a blockchain that allows students, educators, and institutions to manage and interact with educational data without a central authority, ensuring transparency and security in the educational process.

QUIZ:

Crypto and Blockchain in Education

1. **What is blockchain technology, and how is it being integrated into educational institutions?**

   a) It is a centralized database used to store academic records manually.

   b) It is a decentralized digital ledger used for secure and transparent management of student records and administrative tasks.

   c) It is a private server owned by universities to share grades.

   d) It is a digital platform designed solely for issuing printed diplomas.

2. **How do digital credentials differ from traditional credentials, and what advantages do they offer?**

   a) They are easily lost and hard to verify.

   b) They are handwritten certificates stored in vaults.

   c) They are stored on a blockchain, making them tamper-proof, easily verifiable, and globally accessible.

   d) They are encrypted diplomas that cannot be shared.

3. **What role does cryptography play in blockchain technology?**

   a) It decorates blockchain certificates with graphics.

   b) It secures data and transactions on the blockchain, protecting information from unauthorized access.

   c) It erases student records after graduation.

   d) It makes student information public and editable.

4. **Why is hands-on training important in blockchain education?**

a) It teaches students how to buy cryptocurrencies.

b) It provides practical experience in blockchain development and real-world applications.

c) It focuses on building new centralized banks.

d) It reduces the need for coding skills.

5. **What are some examples of blockchain being used in educational institutions today?**

a) Harvard and Oxford using blockchain for cafeteria management.

b) University of Nicosia and MIT using blockchain to manage records and issue digital diplomas.

c) High schools mining Bitcoin for class projects.

d) Colleges selling NFTs instead of issuing degrees.

6. **How do smart contracts improve administrative efficiency in education?**

a) They create physical transcripts faster.

b) They automate tasks like admissions, financial aid processing, and course registration, reducing errors and workload.

c) They manually verify student information.

d) They limit student access to academic records.

7. **What is a decentralized application (dApp), and how is it relevant to blockchain education?**

a) A centralized server for classroom attendance.

b) A blockchain-based software tool allowing students, educators, and institutions to manage educational data transparently and securely.

c) A government database for tax filing.

d) A mobile game designed for university students.

8. **What are the benefits of industry partnerships in blockchain education?**

a) They sell educational merchandise to students.

b) They allow companies to control academic curricula.

c) They provide students with real-world blockchain project experience and industry insights.

d) They limit student access to new technologies.

☑ ANSWER KEY WITH DETAILED EXPLANATIONS

1. **b) It is a decentralized digital ledger used for secure and transparent management of student records and administrative tasks.**

   Explanation:

   Blockchain enables educational institutions to securely store academic records, automate administrative functions, and improve transparency, all without relying on a single centralized authority.

2. **c) They are stored on a blockchain, making them tamper-proof, easily verifiable, and globally accessible.**

   Explanation:

   Digital credentials eliminate the risks of forgery and loss. They can be easily shared with employers and institutions worldwide, providing a secure and efficient way to verify academic achievements.

3. **b) It secures data and transactions on the blockchain, protecting information from unauthorized access.**

   Explanation:

   Cryptography encrypts sensitive data on the blockchain, ensuring that student records and transactions remain confidential and tamper-proof.

4. **b) It provides practical experience in blockchain development and real-world applications.**

    Explanation:

    Hands-on experiences, such as hackathons and blockchain internships, help students apply theoretical knowledge, preparing them for actual careers in the blockchain and crypto industries.

5. **b) University of Nicosia and MIT using blockchain to manage records and issue digital diplomas.**

    Explanation:

    These institutions are pioneers in using blockchain to issue verifiable digital diplomas and streamline record management, showcasing real-world educational applications of the technology.

6. **b) They automate tasks like admissions, financial aid processing, and course registration, reducing errors and workload.**

    Explanation:

    Smart contracts execute predefined administrative functions automatically, saving time, reducing human error, and improving the overall efficiency of educational operations.

7. **b) A blockchain-based software tool allowing students, educators, and institutions to manage educational data transparently and securely.**

    Explanation:

    dApps provide decentralized control over educational activities, removing the need for a central authority and enhancing data transparency, integrity, and user trust.

8. c) They provide students with real-world blockchain project experience and industry insights.

Explanation:

Industry partnerships connect students with active blockchain companies, offering valuable hands-on experience and insights into real-world
blockchain applications, boosting students' employability and understanding.

CHAPTER 12

CASE STUDIES AND SUCCESS STORIES

Key Points

- Successful Blockchain Projects
- Cryptocurrency Adoption Worldwide
- Lessons Learned from Early Adopters
- Overcoming Challenges in Blockchain and Cryptocurrency Adoption

CONTENT

Successful Blockchain Projects

Blockchain technology has seen several successful implementations across various industries, demonstrating its transformative potential. One notable case is IBM's Food Trust, a blockchain platform used to trace the origin of food products from farm to table. This system enhances transparency and efficiency by allowing consumers and companies to track food production, reducing food fraud and contamination. The Food Trust has been adopted by industry giants like Walmart and Nestlé, showcasing how blockchain can improve the efficiency of complex supply chains.

Another successful project is VeChain, a blockchain-based platform designed for supply chain logistics. It provides real-time tracking, which enables businesses to monitor their products' movement across borders and within industries. VeChain's use of Internet of Things (IoT) devices further enhances its capacity to provide tamper-proof data, making it a trusted solution for companies handling sensitive products, such as pharmaceuticals and luxury goods.

Ethereum has also set a strong precedent for blockchain's success. Its use in enabling smart contracts and decentralized applications (dApps) has revolutionized industries such as finance, gaming, and identity verification. Ethereum has empowered developers worldwide to create innovative solutions for real-world problems by leveraging blockchain's secure, decentralized infrastructure.

Cryptocurrency Adoption Worldwide

Cryptocurrency adoption has accelerated worldwide, with ownership now estimated at over **659 million people**, a **13% increase** from the previous year. While growth is happening across nearly every continent, adoption remains **uneven and deeply influenced by local conditions**—from inflation and financial instability to regulation and tech innovation.

In **countries like Venezuela and Nigeria**, where economic instability, currency devaluation, and hyperinflation are part of daily life, cryptocurrencies such as **Bitcoin** and **stablecoins** have emerged as lifelines. Citizens in these regions use digital assets to store wealth securely, shield their savings from inflation, and move money across borders without depending on unreliable or restrictive banking systems. In these economies, crypto isn't about speculation—it's about **survival** and **financial freedom**.

On the other hand, **developed nations** are adopting cryptocurrency for very different reasons. In **Japan**, a progressive and clearly defined regulatory framework has fostered trust and consumer confidence, making it one of the most crypto-friendly nations in Asia. **South Korea** boasts one of the highest crypto users per capita concentrations, supported by advanced technology infrastructure, local exchanges, and an engaged public sector. Both countries view cryptocurrency as part of a broader fintech evolution.

In the **United States**, adoption has transitioned from niche to mainstream. Companies like **PayPal**, **Tesla**, **Square**, and **Coinbase** have normalized digital assets for millions of Americans. Whether it's using Bitcoin to make purchases, integrating crypto wallets into apps, or offering crypto-backed investments, major players are driving public awareness and institutional trust. At the same time, U.S. regulatory bodies such as the **SEC**, **CFTC**, and **IRS** are working to establish more straightforward guidelines, prompting national conversations around **consumer protection, compliance, taxation,** and **responsible innovation**. While the approach is measured, the U.S. remains a leading force in **shaping the global crypto policy landscape**.

U.S. Government Agencies Involved in Crypto Regulation:

- **SEC – Securities and Exchange Commission**
  The SEC oversees the securities markets and protects investors. In the crypto space, the SEC evaluates whether certain digital assets (like some tokens) qualify as securities and thus fall under its regulation.

- **CFTC – Commodity Futures Trading Commission**

  Regulates derivatives markets, including futures and commodities. The CFTC has claimed oversight over cryptocurrencies like Bitcoin and Ethereum when they're traded as commodities.

- **IRS – Internal Revenue Service**

  The U.S. federal agency responsible for tax collection and enforcement. The IRS treats cryptocurrency as property for tax purposes, meaning users must report capital gains and losses from crypto transactions.

Globally, countries like **India, Brazil, Turkey, the Philippines, and Ukraine are seeing sharp increases in crypto use,** often driven by **remittances, e-commerce, hedging against inflation**, or the rise of **play-to-earn** gaming economies. In some areas, mobile-first access to financial apps has allowed digital wallets to leapfrog traditional banking entirely.

Lessons Learned from Early Adopters

The first wave of countries, companies, and platforms to embrace blockchain and cryptocurrency has given the world a wealth of insight—what works, what doesn't, and what must evolve for this technology to scale responsibly.

🏛 Regulatory Clarity: The Cornerstone of Innovation

One of the most important lessons from early adopters is the critical role of regulatory clarity. Countries like Malta and Switzerland set the tone early by crafting crypto-friendly regulations. Malta, branding itself the "Blockchain Island," attracted a surge of blockchain startups and exchanges by offering clear compliance frameworks, tax advantages, and legal certainty.

Switzerland, particularly through its Crypto Valley in Zug, became a global hub for blockchain innovation thanks to its progressive policies and fintech-friendly environment. These examples underscore a key point: when governments provide clarity and support, innovation thrives.

Conversely, inconsistent or overly aggressive regulation has caused major setbacks in other parts of the world. China, once a leader in Bitcoin mining, enacted sweeping bans on crypto trading and mining, pushing major firms to relocate to countries like Kazakhstan, the United States, and El Salvador, where conditions were more favorable. These moves disrupted operations and reshaped the global distribution of crypto infrastructure—especially Bitcoin's hash rate.

In the United States, although regulatory discussions have been ongoing, progress has been incremental. The involvement of the SEC (Securities and Exchange Commission), CFTC (Commodity Futures Trading Commission), and IRS (Internal Revenue Service) has created overlapping jurisdictional challenges. However, recent bipartisan pushes for comprehensive digital asset legislation have signaled a shift toward more stable and actionable policy.

Scalability and Infrastructure: More Than Just Speed

Early adopters also revealed that while blockchain is revolutionary, its infrastructure must evolve to meet demand. One major example is Ethereum. Launched as a decentralized platform for smart contracts and decentralized applications (dApps), Ethereum's popularity exposed scalability issues—particularly during network congestion spikes, which drove gas fees to unsustainable levels.

This led to the much-anticipated launch of Ethereum 2.0, which transitioned the network from proof-of-work to proof-of-stake, aiming to drastically reduce energy consumption and improve transaction through-put. Meanwhile, Layer 2 solutions like Optimism, Arbitrum, and Polygon have emerged to offload pressure from the main chain, allowing for faster and cheaper transactions.

The importance of scalability has also fueled the rise of alternative blockchains like Solana, Avalanche, and Cardano, each promising unique solutions to the blockchain trilemma: security, scalability, and decentralization.

User Education: The Gateway to Mass Adoption

Another key takeaway from early adopters is the power of user education. Cryptocurrency and blockchain remain complex, even intimidating, to the average consumer. Platforms that invested early in educating their users, like Coinbase with its "Learn & Earn" program, have seen significantly higher engagement, retention, and trust.

Today, education goes beyond just wallets and exchanges. It includes understanding topics like self-custody, private keys, regulatory risks, DeFi (Decentralized Finance), NFTs, and wallet security. Projects and communities that proactively explain these concepts without hype are building stronger, more resilient user bases.

Educational institutions are also catching on. Universities around the world now offer blockchain courses and certifications. Organizations like the Digital Assets Council of Financial Professionals (DACFP) are training traditional financial advisors to understand crypto, so they can responsibly guide clients in this emerging asset class.

Key Takeaway:

Early adoption brought excitement—but also friction. Those who succeeded didn't just bet on the technology. They built support systems: clear rules, scalable infrastructure, and education for the people. The next generation of crypto growth will depend on how well we learn from these pioneers—and how intentionally we apply those lessons in the years ahead..

Overcoming Challenges in Blockchain and Cryptocurrency Adoption

While the potential of blockchain and cryptocurrencies is evident, several challenges hinder widespread adoption. Scalability remains a significant issue for many blockchain platforms, particularly those like Ethereum, which process thousands of transactions daily. Layer 2 solutions and new consensus mechanisms such as proof-of-stake aim to solve these issues, enabling blockchains to handle larger transaction volumes while maintaining security and decentralization.

Another challenge is regulatory uncertainty, particularly in regions where governments have yet to establish a clear stance on digital currencies. In the absence of clear regulations, businesses and individuals face uncertainty, which discourages them from adopting or investing in blockchain technologies. A solution to this issue is the creation of regulatory sandboxes, which allow companies to experiment with blockchain innovations in a controlled environment without facing immediate legal hurdles.

Lastly, security concerns such as smart contract vulnerabilities and potential hacking incidents remain a threat. Hackers have exploited security weaknesses in decentralized applications and cryptocurrency exchanges, leading to losses worth millions of dollars. A greater focus on security audits, third-party reviews, and the use of advanced encryption methods can help mitigate these risks.

SUMMARY

Blockchain technology has made significant inroads across various industries, with projects like IBM's Food Trust and Ethereum leading the way. These innovations highlight blockchain's potential to revolutionize supply chain management, decentralized applications, and financial services. However, challenges such as scalability, regulatory uncertainty, and security concerns remain hurdles to widespread adoption. Early adopters like Switzerland and Malta have demonstrated the importance of clear regulatory frameworks, while countries facing economic instability have embraced cryptocurrencies to stabilize their economies. Overcoming these challenges will require a concerted effort from governments, industry leaders, and technologists, but the promise of blockchain and cryptocurrency remains strong.

QUOTE

"Blockchain's potential for disruption goes beyond just finance; it will touch every aspect of our lives where transparency, security, and decentralization are essential."

— Don Tapscott

DEFINITIONS

1. **Supply Chain Blockchain**: A type of blockchain used in industries to track products throughout their lifecycle, ensuring transparency and authenticity. For instance, IBM's Food Trust uses this technology to trace the origin of food products, enhancing safety and reducing fraud.

2. **VeChain**: A blockchain platform specifically designed to improve supply chain management through real-time tracking, providing transparency, and preventing counterfeit goods in industries like pharmaceuticals and luxury items.

3. **Smart Contracts**: Self-executing agreements that run on a blockchain. They automatically enforce the terms of a contract when conditions are met, removing the need for intermediaries. In the context of case studies, Ethereum is a major platform enabling smart contracts across industries like finance and gaming.

4. **Regulatory Clarity**: The establishment of clear guidelines by governments for the use and trading of blockchain and cryptocurrency technologies. Countries like Malta and Switzerland have implemented regulatory frameworks that encourage blockchain innovation while ensuring legal compliance.

5. **Economic Instability Adoption**: The use of cryptocurrencies in countries facing economic challenges, such as Venezuela and Nigeria, where hyperinflation and currency devaluation have made digital currencies a more stable alternative.

6. **Decentralized Applications (dApps)**: Applications built on blockchain platforms like Ethereum that function without centralized control. These applications span industries from finance to supply chains, offering decentralized solutions for real-world problems.

7. **Scalability Solutions**: Technologies developed to address the issue of increasing transaction volumes on blockchain platforms. Ethereum's transition to Ethereum 2.0, which uses Proof-of-Stake (PoS), is an example of efforts to scale the network to accommodate more users.

8. **Regulatory Sandbox**: A framework allowing startups to test block-chain and crypto innovations under the supervision of regulatory bodies without immediately facing full regulatory scrutiny. It has been successfully used in countries like Malta to foster blockchain development.

QUIZ

Case Studies and Success Stories

1. **What are some successful blockchain projects that have revolutionized industries?**

   a) IBM's Food Trust and VeChain for supply chains, and Ethereum for decentralized applications and smart contracts

   b) Bitcoin Cash and Litecoin for healthcare services

   c) PayPal and Western Union for logistics

   d) Instagram and Spotify for food production tracking

2. **How has cryptocurrency adoption differed across various regions?**

   a) Every country adopted crypto at the same speed and for the same reasons

   b) Countries like Venezuela and Nigeria adopted crypto for survival, while Japan and South Korea adopted it through regulatory support

   c) Only developed countries use cryptocurrency regularly

   d) Cryptocurrency is mainly used for gaming purposes globally

3. **What key lessons have early adopters of blockchain technology learned?**

   a) That government bans are necessary for innovation

   b) That regulatory clarity, scalability, and user education are crucial for success

   c) That rapid adoption without regulations is the best approach

   d) That blockchain adoption works best with minimal public involvement

4. **What are the primary challenges in achieving widespread blockchain adoption?**

   a) Marketing failures and branding issues

   b) Scalability, regulatory uncertainty, and security concerns

   c) Lack of hardware devices to support blockchain

   d) Shortage of blockchain developers worldwide

5. **How can regulatory sandboxes help in blockchain innovation?**

   a) By allowing startups to bypass all regulations permanently

   b) By allowing companies to experiment with blockchain technologies in a controlled, flexible environment

   c) By shutting down experimental blockchain projects early

   d) By making all blockchain projects fully decentralized immediately

6. **What role does security play in the adoption of decentralized applications?**

   a) Minimal role, since blockchain is inherently secure

   b) It is critical, as vulnerabilities in smart contracts and hacking incidents can damage trust and cause financial losses

   c) Security only matters during the initial launch phase

   d) Smart contracts do not require any additional security measures

☑ ANSWER KEY WITH DETAILED EXPLANATIONS

1. a) IBM's Food Trust and VeChain for supply chains, and Ethereum for decentralized applications and smart contracts

    Explanation:

    IBM's Food Trust and VeChain have demonstrated how blockchain can transform supply chain management by increasing transparency and reducing fraud. Meanwhile, Ethereum has pioneered the development of decentralized applications (dApps) and smart contracts across industries such as finance, gaming, and identity verification.

2. b) Countries like Venezuela and Nigeria adopted crypto for survival, while Japan and South Korea adopted it through regulatory support

    Explanation:

    In countries experiencing economic instability, like Venezuela and Nigeria, citizens turned to cryptocurrencies as a store of value and a means of survival. In contrast, nations like Japan and South Korea, with strong regulatory frameworks, have integrated cryptocurrency into mainstream finance and innovation sectors.

3. b) That regulatory clarity, scalability, and user education are crucial for success

    Explanation:

    Early adopters showed that for blockchain technologies to thrive, clear regulations, scalable infrastructure, and robust user education are essential. Countries like Malta and Switzerland succeeded by providing these support systems, while inconsistent regulation caused setbacks elsewhere.

4. **b) Scalability, regulatory uncertainty, and security concerns**
    Explanation:
    Blockchain's mass adoption faces hurdles like network congestion (scalability issues), unclear regulatory environments, and persistent security threats, particularly in decentralized applications where smart contract vulnerabilities can lead to major financial losses.

5. **b) By allowing companies to experiment with blockchain technologies in a controlled, flexible environment**
    Explanation:
    Regulatory sandboxes provide a safe space for blockchain startups to innovate while still under the supervision of regulators. This approach encourages innovation while helping governments understand new technologies without immediately imposing restrictive regulations.

6. **b) It is critical, as vulnerabilities in smart contracts and hacking incidents can damage trust and cause financial losses**
    Explanation:
    Security is paramount for decentralized applications (dApps). Hacking incidents and vulnerabilities in smart contracts can erode user trust and result in massive financial losses, threatening the broader adoption of blockchain technologies. Thorough auditing and security testing are essential.

CHAPTER 13

THE FUTURE OF MONEY: PREDICTIONS AND SPECULATIONS

Key Points

- Potential Scenarios for Global Financial Systems
- The Role of Central Bank Digital Currencies (CBDCs)
- Long-Term Implications for Society
- Innovations to Watch

CONTENT

Potential Scenarios for Global Financial Systems

As the world moves toward an increasingly digitized financial landscape, the future of global financial systems is expected to involve a combination of both centralized and decentralized solutions. Here are several potential outcomes:

1. **Dominance of Digital Currencies**: As individuals and businesses continue to adopt digital currencies for transactions, we could see a decline in the use of physical cash. With the growing use of digital wallets and decentralized finance (DeFi) platforms, reliance on traditional banking systems may decrease.

2. **Centralization through CBDCs**: Central bank digital currencies (CBDCs) present an opportunity for governments to digitize their fiat currencies, ensuring they retain control over monetary policies while offering efficient and transparent payment solutions.

3. **Global Adoption of Stablecoins**: Stablecoins, which are pegged to traditional assets like national currencies, might emerge as intermediaries between the crypto world and the fiat currency system, providing a bridge that allows seamless international transactions without the volatility of other cryptocurrencies.

4. **Integration of Blockchain in Traditional Finance**: Rather than a complete replacement of traditional systems, blockchain technology could enhance financial infrastructures by speeding up processes like clearing, settlement, and international remittances. Banks may adopt distributed ledger technology (DLT) to increase efficiency, transparency, and security.

5. **A Hybrid System**: The future might bring a hybrid financial ecosystem where both decentralized financial services and traditional financial institutions co-exist, offering consumers and businesses more options. In such a system, blockchain technology and traditional banking structures might complement each other, striking a balance between security, efficiency, and accessibility.

The Role of Central Bank Digital Currencies (CBDCs)

CBDCs represent one of the most significant innovations in the future of money, with several countries already in the process of developing or piloting these currencies:

- **Efficiency and Security**: CBDCs combine the speed and security of digital currencies with the stability of government-backed fiat currencies. By digitizing national currencies, governments can reduce the reliance on physical cash, increase transparency, and offer faster transaction processing.

- **Enhanced Monetary Policy Tools**: Central banks could gain more control over the money supply with CBDCs. Tools like negative interest rates and direct transfers could be implemented more efficiently, stimulating economic activity or controlling inflation in a way not possible with traditional cash.

- **Financial Inclusion**: CBDCs could provide an entry point to formal financial systems for unbanked populations. In developing nations, individuals without traditional banking access could participate in the digital economy via mobile wallets connected to a CBDC system.

- **Geopolitical Influence**: Countries that launch successful CBDCs may enhance their geopolitical standing. For instance, China's digital yuan could challenge the U.S. dollar's dominance in global trade, while the Bahamas has already launched its Sand Dollar as a digital currency alternative.

Long-Term Implications for Society

As digital currencies continue to gain traction, their long-term societal implications will become more apparent:

1. **Governance and Regulation**: Governments will need to implement new frameworks to regulate digital currencies, including oversight for CBDCs and decentralized finance. There will be an ongoing balancing act between promoting innovation and maintaining financial stability.

2. **Privacy and Surveillance**: While blockchain offers transparent transactions, it also raises privacy concerns. Governments, using CBDCs, may gain more control over financial surveillance, sparking debates over privacy rights versus security needs.

3. **Economic Inclusion**: By removing intermediaries, digital currencies have the potential to democratize financial services, especially for the unbanked. However, the digital divide—where some populations lack access to technology—remains a challenge.

4. **Job Displacement**: With the automation of financial processes and the rise of decentralized platforms, traditional financial institutions may see reduced demand for certain roles. This could lead to job displacement in sectors like banking and finance.

5. **Cross-Border Trade**: Digital currencies, especially stablecoins and CBDCs, can streamline international trade by reducing the need for currency conversion and intermediaries. This could lead to faster, more affordable cross-border transactions, changing how global trade operates.

Innovations to Watch

Several innovations are poised to shape the future of money and digital transactions:

- **Programmable Money**: Digital currencies are programmable, meaning they can be designed to execute specific rules or conditions. For instance, smart contracts can automatically facilitate transactions such as tax payments or welfare distribution when predefined criteria are met.

- **Quantum-Resistant Cryptography**: As quantum computing technology advances, it poses a potential risk to the cryptographic methods currently used in blockchain systems. Quantum-resistant cryptography is being developed to protect blockchain networks from these future attacks. Lattice-based cryptography and hash-based signatures are some of the approaches being explored to ensure blockchain security in a post-quantum world.

- **Decentralized Autonomous Organizations (DAOs)**: DAOs are self-governing organizations built on blockchain technology. These entities operate through smart contracts and are governed by their members, offering an innovative approach to decentralized governance in various sectors, including finance and business.

- **AI-Driven Financial Systems**: The integration of artificial intelligence into financial systems will drive more efficient decision-making. AI could analyze vast amounts of financial data, predict market trends, and execute trades or manage portfolios with minimal human intervention.

SUMMARY

The future of money will likely be defined by a convergence of traditional financial systems and cutting-edge digital innovations. Central bank digital currencies (CBDCs) and decentralized finance (DeFi) are expected to play critical roles, offering secure, efficient, and transparent financial services. As quantum-resistant cryptography becomes essential to secure blockchain systems against potential quantum computing threats, the evolution of money will continue to shape global economies. The implications of these innovations will affect everything from financial governance and regulation to economic inclusion and cross-border trade.

QUOTE

"The future of money is digital, and blockchain will be at the heart of this transformation."

– Christine Lagarde, President of the European Central Bank

DEFINITIONS

1. **Central Bank Digital Currency (CBDC)**: A digital version of government-backed fiat currency issued by central banks, offering the efficiency of cryptocurrencies while maintaining monetary control.

2. **Stablecoin**: A type of cryptocurrency that is pegged to a stable asset, such as a fiat currency or commodity, to reduce volatility.

3. **Decentralized Finance (DeFi)**: Financial services provided on decentralized blockchain networks, eliminating the need for traditional intermediaries like banks.

4. **Quantum-Resistant Cryptography**: Cryptographic methods designed to withstand attacks from quantum computers, ensuring the continued security of blockchain systems in a post-quantum world.

5. **Smart Contract**: A self-executing contract with the terms of the agreement directly written into code, facilitating automated and trustless transactions.

6. **Decentralized Autonomous Organization (DAO)**: An organization governed by smart contracts on a blockchain, where decision-making is decentralized and carried out by its members.

7. **Programmable Money**: Digital currency that can be programmed to execute specific tasks or conditions automatically, such as making payments or distributing funds.

8. **Blockchain Interoperability**: The ability of different blockchain systems to interact and share data seamlessly, enabling more cohesive financial and technological ecosystems.

QUIZ

Chapter 13 – The Future of Money: Predictions and Speculations

1. **What is a Central Bank Digital Currency (CBDC), and how could it change traditional financial systems?**

   a) A decentralized cryptocurrency not backed by any government

   b) A digital form of government-backed currency offering efficient and transparent transactions

   c) A private company's token designed for online shopping

   d) A loyalty points system used by banks

2. **How can Decentralized Finance (DeFi) improve financial services?**

   a) By creating additional intermediaries

   b) By allowing peer-to-peer financial transactions without traditional banks

   c) By increasing government control over financial markets

   d) By requiring identification at every transaction

3. **What are stablecoins, and how do they differ from other cryptocurrencies?**

   a) They are cryptocurrencies without any backing or asset tie

   b) They are cryptocurrencies pegged to stable assets like fiat currencies to reduce volatility

   c) They are tokens only usable in online games

   d) They fluctuate more than Bitcoin

4. **Why is quantum-resistant cryptography important for the future of blockchain security?**

   a) Because it allows faster blockchain mining

   b) Because it prevents hacking by future quantum computers

   c) Because it increases transaction fees

   d) Because it decentralizes finance systems further

5. **What role do Decentralized Autonomous Organizations (DAOs) play in future governance?**

   a) They reinforce centralized control over decision-making

   b) They enable decentralized governance through smart contracts

   c) They regulate banks and traditional financial institutions

   d) They create government-backed cryptocurrency exchanges

6. **How could programmable money transform the way transactions are conducted?**

   a) By making transactions anonymous and unverifiable

   b) By executing automatic transactions like welfare distribution or tax collection based on pre-set conditions

   c) By creating physical cash alternatives only

   d) By requiring multiple manual approvals for simple transactions

7. **What are the potential benefits of integrating AI into financial systems?**

   a) AI reduces the need for digital records

   b) AI analyzes large datasets, predicts trends, and manages financial activities efficiently

   c) AI increases the reliance on manual oversight in trading

   d) AI slows down blockchain confirmations to increase accuracy

8. How might blockchain interoperability shape the future of global financial systems?

   a) By preventing blockchains from sharing data with each other

   b) By allowing different blockchain networks to communicate and work together

   c) By replacing blockchains with traditional ledgers

   d) By ensuring that all currencies remain localized and isolated

☑ ANSWER KEY WITH DETAILED EXPLANATIONS

1. b) A digital form of government-backed currency offering efficient and transparent transactions

   Explanation:

   CBDCs combine the advantages of digital payment systems with the trust and backing of government-issued fiat money. They can increase efficiency in transactions, boost transparency, and allow governments to modernize the monetary system while maintaining control over monetary policy.

2. b) By allowing peer-to-peer financial transactions without traditional banks

   Explanation:

   DeFi platforms enable direct interaction between users, eliminating intermediaries like banks or brokers. This lowers transaction costs, increases financial accessibility globally, and empowers users to control their own assets through decentralized protocols.

3. **b) They are cryptocurrencies pegged to stable assets like fiat currencies to reduce volatility**

    Explanation:

    Stablecoins provide a bridge between traditional finance and the crypto world. By being pegged to assets like the U.S. dollar or gold, they maintain a consistent value, making them ideal for everyday transactions, cross-border payments, and trading stability.

4. **b) Because it prevents hacking by future quantum computers**

    Explanation:

    Quantum computers could easily break the cryptographic techniques that secure current blockchain systems. Quantum-resistant cryptography is essential to protect sensitive data and ensure that blockchain networks remain secure against future quantum threats.

5. **b) They enable decentralized governance through smart contracts**

    Explanation:

    DAOs operate without a centralized leadership structure. Decisions are made collectively by members who vote using smart contracts, allowing for transparent, community-driven governance models that can transform industries like finance, business, and social organizations.

6. **b) By executing automatic transactions like welfare distribution or tax collection based on pre-set conditions**

    Explanation:

    Programmable money allows governments and businesses to automate payments based on rules encoded into the digital currency itself. This can streamline complex transactions, reduce administrative errors, and make processes like benefit distribution faster and more efficient.

7. **b) AI analyzes large datasets, predicts trends, and manages financial activities efficiently**

   Explanation:

   AI's ability to process massive volumes of financial data enables faster decision-making, more accurate market predictions, and better risk management strategies. In finance, AI can optimize trading strategies, automate portfolio management, and detect fraud with high precision.

8. **b) By allowing different blockchain networks to communicate and work together**

   Explanation:

   Blockchain interoperability is crucial for building a seamless financial ecosystem where assets and data can move freely across different platforms. It promotes collaboration between different blockchains, boosts efficiency, and creates a more connected global economy.

CHAPTER 14

A VISION FOR THE FUTURE:
CRYPTO, AI, AND BLOCKCHAIN

Key Points

- Synergies Between Crypto, AI, and Blockchain
- Potential Innovations and Applications
- Ethical and Societal Implications
- Future Technological Integrations

CONTENT

Synergies Between Crypto, AI, and Blockchain

At the intersection of cryptocurrency, artificial intelligence (AI), and blockchain, the convergence of these technologies promises to redefine industries and transform the way we interact with technology. Each of these innovations has unique strengths, and together, they offer exciting possibilities. By blending AI's capability in data processing with blockchain's security and transparency, and crypto's decentralized approach to financial systems, the combined potential could dramatically shift industries from finance to healthcare.

Blockchain's Trustless Environment: Blockchain provides a decentralized and trustless system where interactions occur without intermediaries like banks or governments. AI can enhance this environment by automating decision-making processes through sophisticated data analysis. AI and blockchain could allow for smarter smart contracts that adjust autonomously based on AI analysis of market trends. For example, decentralized finance (DeFi) platforms could dynamically adjust interest rates in real-time without central oversight, driven by AI analysis.

AI-Driven Blockchain Analytics: AI's ability to analyze large datasets can be invaluable for blockchain applications, particularly for improving security. AI models can be trained to detect suspicious patterns in blockchain transactions, optimizing security in real-time. This can be critical in detecting fraud, improving overall efficiency, and preventing financial crimes within decentralized networks.

AI-Powered Decentralized Governance: Decentralized Autonomous Organizations (DAOs) are blockchain-based organizations that function without central leadership. By incorporating AI into these models, DAOs could operate more efficiently, making decisions based on AI-driven data insights. The entire governance process could become automated, enhancing operational efficiency and removing the need for human intermediaries.

Privacy-Preserving AI and Blockchain

Privacy is a core concern in both AI and blockchain. Blockchain's transparency often conflicts with AI's need for vast amounts of data. Privacy-preserving AI, powered by blockchain, can help balance the need for data with privacy protections. Techniques such as **zero-knowledge proofs** (ZKPs) and **homomorphic encryption** allow AI models to analyze encrypted data without revealing sensitive information. This fusion could create a future where blockchain ensures that data is tamper-proof, while AI processes it without violating privacy.

For example, in healthcare, blockchain can store sensitive medical records, while AI analyzes the encrypted data to recommend personalized treatments without exposing patient information.

Blockchain-Enhanced Machine Learning

Another exciting synergy between AI and blockchain is **blockchain-enhanced machine learning**. In this model, blockchain is used to manage and track machine learning models. For instance, decentralized AI marketplaces could be created where individuals and companies can share their datasets securely on the blockchain, allowing AI developers to access and train their models on this data while ensuring data ownership and integrity.

These decentralized AI marketplaces would allow for data exchange without needing centralized entities to control the data, helping democratize access to high-quality datasets. This would be particularly useful in industries like autonomous driving, where machine learning models require vast amounts of data for training.

AI in Blockchain-Powered Governance Models

As the use of blockchain technology extends to government systems, **AI-driven governance models** present an opportunity for transparency and efficiency. In this context, governments could use blockchain to ensure tamper-proof voting systems, and AI could be applied to analyze voter preferences and behavior to make governance more dynamic and responsive. For example, smart contracts could be used to allocate public resources efficiently, based on AI assessments of societal needs.

Furthermore, in corporate governance, **AI-enhanced DAOs** could provide transparency and fairness in decision-making, as AI systems analyze data trends and predict outcomes, ensuring that decentralized entities can function more smoothly.

Potential Innovations and Applications

AI-Enhanced Supply Chains: Blockchain has already started revolutionizing supply chains by offering greater transparency and traceability. Adding AI to the mix could enhance the decision-making process across the supply chain. AI could predict demand, adjust production schedules, and optimize shipping routes by processing blockchain-verified data. The result could be fully autonomous supply chains, capable of making decisions based on real-time data.

Decentralized AI Marketplaces: Blockchain could provide a platform for decentralized AI marketplaces where individuals could offer their data for AI training in exchange for cryptocurrency. This would allow for more democratized access to AI development and help eliminate the current data silos that large corporations often maintain.

AI-Powered Financial Markets: In the realm of decentralized finance (DeFi), AI could automate complex financial decisions, making autonomous trading more efficient. For example, AI algorithms could rebalance portfolios or make investment recommendations based on user preferences and financial goals, all executed autonomously on the blockchain.

Ethical and Societal Implications

The fusion of AI and blockchain brings about significant ethical challenges:

Data Ownership and Privacy: As AI requires vast amounts of data, the issue of who owns the data becomes a significant concern. Blockchain offers the potential for individuals to retain ownership of their data, but how AI interacts with this data is a question that needs to be addressed to avoid privacy violations.

Job Displacement: As AI and blockchain automate more industries, there is a risk of job displacement. Smart contracts and autonomous DAOs could eliminate the need for human intermediaries in sectors like finance, supply chain management, and even governance. Societal efforts will need to focus on reskilling and transitioning the workforce to the digital economy.

Accountability in Decentralized Governance: DAOs and decentralized governance models present accountability issues. If a DAO mismanages funds or makes a harmful decision, who is responsible? As AI takes on more decision-making roles, it becomes challenging to hold any entity accountable for mistakes or unethical outcomes.

Future Technological Integrations

Blockchain and AI in Smart Cities: As cities become smarter, AI and blockchain will be crucial in managing and securing data. AI could handle real-time data analysis for traffic management, energy consumption, and even public safety, while blockchain ensures the data's integrity and security.

AI-Powered Oracles for Smart Contracts: Oracles are necessary for feeding real-world data into blockchain systems. AI could make these oracles more accurate and efficient, automating data collection and verification processes that allow smart contracts to execute reliably.

Tokenized AI Models: The future could see AI models tokenized on the blockchain, where developers can buy or rent these models to build AI-driven applications. This would create a new marketplace for AI development and innovation.

SUMMARY

The convergence of AI, blockchain, and cryptocurrency represents a transformative moment in technology, offering groundbreaking possibilities across industries such as healthcare, governance, finance, education, and beyond. Together, these three forces are not just enhancing individual sectors but reshaping the very architecture of how information, value, and trust are created and exchanged globally.

Blockchain's unparalleled security, transparency, and ability to decentralize control provide the infrastructure needed for trustless systems, where intermediaries are no longer necessary. Artificial intelligence brings powerful data-processing and decision-making capabilities that can automate complex tasks, detect patterns humans may miss, and optimize systems in real-time. Cryptocurrency introduces a decentralized financial framework that empowers individuals, promotes financial inclusion, and facilitates peer-to-peer value exchange without relying on traditional banking structures.

When combined, these technologies offer the potential for revolutionary applications: smarter decentralized finance (DeFi) systems that can autonomously adjust based on market conditions, decentralized AI marketplaces that democratize access to innovation, blockchain-anchored healthcare systems that protect patient privacy while enabling precision treatments, transparent governance models free from corruption, and intelligent supply chains capable of optimizing themselves dynamically.

However, these incredible opportunities come with significant ethical, social, and regulatory challenges that must be carefully addressed. Issues such as data privacy, security, algorithmic bias, accountability in decentralized governance, and the risk of exacerbating inequality demand proactive planning and international cooperation. As AI and blockchain automate more sectors, societies must also focus on preparing workers for a changing economy through education and reskilling initiatives.

Ultimately, embracing this new era requires not just technological adoption but also a cultural shift toward responsible innovation, ethical leadership, and inclusive access. If approached thoughtfully, the fusion of blockchain, AI, and cryptocurrency has the power to create a more transparent, equitable, and dynamic future for everyone.

QUOTE

"In the future, digital currencies will likely become part of our daily lives, transforming not only our financial systems but the very fabric of society itself. Technology will not simply change how we transact; it will redefine what money means."

— Christine Lagarde, President of the European Central Bank

DEFINITIONS

1. **Privacy-Preserving AI**: Techniques used to allow AI to analyze data while ensuring the privacy of the information, often using encryption methods like homomorphic encryption or zero-knowledge proofs.

2. **Zero-Knowledge Proofs (ZKPs)**: A cryptographic method where one party can prove to another that a statement is true without revealing any information beyond the validity of the statement itself.

3. **Homomorphic Encryption**: An encryption method that allows computations to be performed on encrypted data without decrypting it first, preserving privacy while enabling AI analytics.

4. **AI-Powered Oracle**: An oracle that uses AI to collect and verify real-world data, which is then provided to smart contracts on the blockchain.

5. **Blockchain-Enhanced Machine Learning**: The use of blockchain to manage and track machine learning models, ensuring transparency, security, and data integrity throughout the model's lifecycle.

6. **Decentralized Autonomous Organization (DAO)**: A blockchain-based organization governed by smart contracts, with decision-making distributed among stakeholders rather than centralized leadership.

7. **Smart Contract**: A self-executing contract with the terms of the agreement directly written into code, allowing for automated transactions without intermediaries.

8. **Decentralized AI Marketplace**: A blockchain-powered platform where users can contribute data or AI models, which can then be accessed by developers or researchers in exchange for tokens.

QUIZ
AI and Blockchain Integration

1. **What role can AI play in enhancing blockchain scalability?**

    a) By reducing the need for consensus

    b) By improving fraud detection and optimizing consensus mechanisms

    c) By making the network more decentralized

    d) By decreasing the number of nodes required

2. **How can privacy-preserving AI be beneficial for blockchain applications?**

    a) It removes the need for encryption

    b) It allows AI to process data without compromising privacy

    c) It eliminates the need for smart contracts

    d) It enhances the security of wallets

3. **What is a decentralized AI marketplace?**

    a) A centralized platform for buying AI models

    b) A marketplace where data for AI training is exchanged using blockchain technology

    c) An AI platform owned by a government

    d) A system where AI runs blockchain networks

4. **How can AI and blockchain transform supply chain management?**

   a) By predicting future trends

   b) By managing contracts in real-time

   c) By automating data processing and increasing transparency through blockchain

   d) By decreasing operational costs

5. **What are DAOs, and how are they different from traditional organizations?**

   a) They are controlled by a central authority

   b) They are governed by a decentralized network and smart contracts

   c) They only exist in the finance sector

   d) They operate without the need for stakeholders

6. **What is the role of AI in privacy-preserving technologies like zero-knowledge proofs (ZKPs)?**

   a) AI replaces blockchain encryption with zero-knowledge proofs

   b) AI enhances the process of verifying data without exposing sensitive information

   c) AI controls blockchain networks directly using ZKPs

   d) AI is unnecessary in privacy-preserving technologies

7. **How can AI-driven blockchain analytics improve security in DeFi platforms?**

   a) By detecting fraudulent behavior and suspicious transaction patterns

   b) By making manual verification easier

   c) By slowing down transaction speeds for better oversight

   d) By eliminating the need for consensus mechanisms

8. Why is blockchain-enhanced machine learning considered revolutionary for AI development?

    a) It makes AI completely autonomous from human input

    b) It ensures secure data management while allowing decentralized access for training models

    c) It speeds up the training of machine learning models by decentralizing power

    d) It makes AI systems unbreakable

9. In what ways could AI-powered oracles be more effective for blockchain networks?

    a) They can autonomously manage blockchain wallets

    b) They can automate the collection and verification of real-world data, improving smart contract execution

    c) They can replace nodes entirely

    d) They remove the need for developers to code smart contracts

10. What is the biggest ethical challenge of combining AI with blockchain in governance systems?

    a) Lack of technological development

    b) Ensuring privacy while maintaining transparency

    c) High energy consumption in AI

    d) Decentralization slows down innovation

☑ ANSWER KEY WITH DETAILED EXPLANATIONS

1. Answer: b) By improving fraud detection and optimizing consensus mechanisms

   Explanation:

   AI can help blockchain networks scale by detecting fraud faster and optimizing how consensus is reached, making the system more efficient and less resource-intensive.

2. Answer: b) It allows AI to process data without compromising privacy

   Explanation:

   Privacy-preserving AI techniques enable data to be processed and learned from without revealing sensitive information, which is critical for blockchain's transparent nature.

3. Answer: b) A marketplace where data for AI training is exchanged using blockchain technology

   Explanation:

   Decentralized AI marketplaces let people share and monetize data for AI models securely using blockchain, avoiding centralized control and encouraging open innovation.

4. Answer: c) By automating data processing and increasing transparency through blockchain

   Explanation:

   Combining AI's automation with blockchain's transparency dramatically improves efficiency and traceability in supply chains.

5.   **Answer: b) They are governed by a decentralized network and smart contracts**

   Explanation:

   Unlike traditional organizations with centralized leadership, DAOs use blockchain and smart contracts to enable decentralized governance by participants.

6.   **Answer: b) AI enhances the process of verifying data without exposing sensitive information**

   Explanation:

   In systems like zero-knowledge proofs, AI can improve verification processes, ensuring data integrity without revealing underlying private information.

7.   **Answer: a) By detecting fraudulent behavior and suspicious transaction patterns**

   Explanation:

   AI can monitor blockchain networks in real-time, spotting irregularities and potential security threats much faster than manual checks.

8.   **Answer: b) It ensures secure data management while allowing decentralized access for training models**

   Explanation:

   Blockchain provides a secure and transparent environment for machine learning, allowing models to be trained collaboratively without compromising the data's privacy or integrity.

9. **Answer: b) They can automate the collection and verification of real-world data, improving smart contract execution**

   Explanation:

   AI-powered oracles can pull real-world data autonomously and feed it into smart contracts, ensuring they execute based on accurate and verified information.

10. **Answer: b) Ensuring privacy while maintaining transparency**

    Explanation:

    Combining AI and blockchain in governance must balance openness (blockchain's strength) with the protection of sensitive data (AI's privacy needs), which remains a major ethical challenge.

CHAPTER 15

DECENTRALIZED GOVERNANCE: BLOCKCHAIN AND THE FUTURE OF ORGANIZATIONS

Key Points

- The Concept of Decentralized Governance and Its Potential in Reshaping Organizations
- Blockchain's Role in Enabling Transparent, Secure, and Tamper-Proof Decision-Making Systems
- Use Cases of Decentralized Autonomous Organizations (DAOs)
- Potential Challenges and Solutions in Implementing Decentralized Governance

The Concept of Decentralized Governance and Its Potential in Reshaping Organizations

Decentralized governance refers to the process of decision-making that distributes authority across multiple participants, rather than consolidating power within a centralized entity. This model offers organizations greater transparency, security, and inclusivity by leveraging blockchain technology to ensure that decisions are made openly and with the participation of all stakeholders.

In decentralized governance, smart contracts play a pivotal role by automating rules and enforcement. When specific conditions are met, these contracts automatically execute decisions, ensuring adherence to the governance framework without the need for human intermediaries. This marks a radical shift from traditional hierarchical governance structures where a select few are responsible for decisions impacting the entire organization. Decentralized governance, especially when integrated with blockchain, offers new opportunities for innovation, financial inclusion, and organizational resilience.

Blockchain's Role in Enabling Transparent, Secure, and Tamper-Proof Decision-Making Systems

Blockchain technology underpins decentralized governance by providing a secure and transparent foundation for decision-making. Each transaction or vote recorded on the blockchain is immutable, meaning it cannot be altered once validated. This eliminates concerns of tampering or fraudulent behavior, as all actions are transparent and verifiable by any participant within the system.

Blockchain also offers decentralized auditability, where all stakeholders can view governance-related data in real-time. This ensures accountability, as decisions can be traced back to their origin, and stakeholders can verify the authenticity of the processes governing the organization. The inherent trustless nature of blockchain means that participants don't need to rely on a central authority to manage their data.

Incorporating blockchain in governance also provides a mechanism to record votes securely. Whether it's organizational decisions or high-level policy enactments, the distributed nature of blockchain ensures that every participant's input is recorded and valued.

Use Cases of Decentralized Autonomous Organizations (DAOs)

Decentralized Autonomous Organizations (DAOs) are perhaps the most well-known example of decentralized governance. DAOs leverage smart contracts to automate decision-making processes, allowing for transparent, consensus-based governance. Each participant in a DAO holds tokens that represent voting power, and decisions are made based on collective votes.

MakerDAO, one of the earliest and most prominent DAOs, governs the DAI stablecoin, which maintains a peg to the U.S. dollar. Decisions related to the development and governance of DAI, including interest rates and collateral types, are made through votes cast by token holders.

Another example of decentralized governance through DAOs is Aragon, a platform that enables users to create and manage DAOs for a variety of purposes. These DAOs can range from managing investment funds to governing communities. With pre-set governance rules encoded into smart contracts, DAOs allow organizations to operate autonomously and without the need for centralized oversight.

Potential Challenges and Solutions in Implementing Decentralized Governance

While decentralized governance offers many benefits, it also presents several challenges. One of the main issues is **scalability**. As the number of participants in a DAO increases, reaching consensus can become more difficult and time-consuming. This can hinder the efficiency of decision-making processes.

Legal recognition is another challenge. Many DAOs operate in a gray area legally, as existing regulatory frameworks do not account for organizations governed by smart contracts. Governments may need to adapt their legal systems to accommodate DAOs and ensure they are compliant with financial and corporate regulations.

Another issue is the **concentration of voting power**. In many DAOs, voting rights are allocated based on token ownership, which can lead to centralization if a few participants own the majority of the tokens. This contradicts the decentralized ethos of DAOs and can create governance imbalances. Potential solutions include implementing quadratic voting, which reduces the influence of token whales by making each additional vote progressively more expensive.

Finally, **decision-making efficiency** can be improved through AI integration. AI can optimize voting systems, automate decision-making processes, and enhance the efficiency of decentralized governance structures. Combining AI with blockchain in governance may create hybrid models that improve decision-making speed while maintaining transparency.

SUMMARY

Decentralized governance, powered by blockchain technology, offers a revolutionary model for organizations by distributing authority, enhancing transparency, and reducing reliance on intermediaries. DAOs serve as a primary example of how decentralized governance can function in practice, with blockchain ensuring that decisions are made openly and securely. While there are challenges such as scalability, legal recognition, and centralization of voting power, solutions such as quadratic voting and AI integration may help address these issues. As blockchain and AI technologies continue to evolve, decentralized governance could become a transformative force in shaping the future of organizations worldwide.

QUOTE

"Whereas most technologies tend to automate workers on the periphery doing menial tasks, blockchains automate away the center. Instead of putting the taxi driver out of a job, blockchain puts Uber out of a job and lets the taxi drivers work with the customer directly."

– Vitalik Buterin, The co-founder of Ethereum

DEFINITIONS

1. **Decentralized Governance**: A system of governance where decision-making authority is distributed among multiple participants rather than centralized within a single entity or organization.

2. **Smart Contract**: Self-executing contracts with the terms of the agreement directly written into code, automating the enforcement of decisions.

3. **Decentralized Autonomous Organization (DAO)**: A blockchain-based organization governed by smart contracts where decision-making is decentralized and conducted through voting by stakeholders.

4. **Consensus Mechanism**: A process used by blockchain networks to achieve agreement on the validity of transactions and governance actions.

5. **Quadratic Voting**: A voting system that allows participants to cast votes, but the cost of each additional vote grows exponentially, reducing the influence of large stakeholders.

6. **Immutability**: The property of blockchain technology that ensures once data is recorded, it cannot be altered or deleted.

7. **Distributed Ledger**: A decentralized database that records transactions and information across multiple locations without a central authority.

8. **Token Governance**: A system in which decisions are made by token holders who vote on proposals based on their share of the tokens.

QUIZ

Decentralized Governance and DAOs

1. What is decentralized governance, and how does it differ from traditional governance?

    a) It centralizes authority among executives.

    b) It distributes decision-making authority among participants.

    c) It uses smart contracts to eliminate governance.

    d) It eliminates the need for decision-making altogether.

2. How does blockchain technology support decentralized governance?

    a) By recording all decisions in an immutable and transparent manner.

    b) By allowing centralized decision-making.

    c) By automating transactions without oversight.

    d) By centralizing all decisions within a DAO.

3. What is a DAO?

    a) A centralized voting organization.

    b) A decentralized organization governed by smart contracts.

    c) A financial institution.

    d) A legal entity that issues tokens.

4. What challenge does the concentration of token ownership in DAOs create?

    a) It makes decision-making faster.

    b) It centralizes governance power.

    c) It increases transparency.

    d) It increases the number of voters.

5. **What is one potential solution to the problem of token centralization in DAOs?**

   a) Token burning.

   b) Centralized governance.

   c) Quadratic voting.

   d) Elimination of tokens.

6. **What are smart contracts primarily used for in DAOs?**

   a) Managing supply chains.

   b) Automating governance decisions.

   c) Centralizing decision-making power.

   d) Selling tokens.

7. **How does decentralized governance improve transparency in organizations?**

   a) By keeping decision-making records private.

   b) By involving fewer people in decision-making.

   c) By making all decisions publicly recorded on a blockchain.

   d) By using a central authority to oversee decisions.

8. **What role do tokens play in decentralized governance?**

   a) They replace traditional currencies in transactions.

   b) They act as voting shares for decision-making.

   c) They are used solely for fundraising.

   d) They eliminate the need for stakeholders.

☑ ANSWER KEY WITH DETAILED EXPLANATIONS

1. **Answer: b) It distributes decision-making authority among participants.**

   Explanation:

   Decentralized governance shifts authority from a small group of executives to all participants in a network or organization, giving everyone a voice in decisions.

2. **Answer: a) By recording all decisions in an immutable and transparent manner.**

   Explanation:

   Blockchain records governance activities on a public ledger that cannot be changed, ensuring transparency and trust in decision-making processes.

3. **Answer: b) A decentralized organization governed by smart contracts.**

   Explanation:

   A DAO (Decentralized Autonomous Organization) uses smart contracts to execute decisions automatically, with governance typically based on token-holder voting.

4. **Answer: b) It centralizes governance power.**

   Explanation:

   If a small group holds most of the tokens, they can dominate voting and decision-making, which undermines the goal of decentralization.

5. **Answer: c) Quadratic voting.**
    Explanation:
    Quadratic voting gives more weight to minority opinions by making each additional vote cost progressively more tokens, reducing the impact of large holders dominating decisions.

6. **Answer: b) Automating governance decisions.**
    Explanation:
    In DAOs, smart contracts automate governance by enforcing voting results and executing decisions without needing manual intervention.

7. **Answer: c) By making all decisions publicly recorded on a blockchain.**
    Explanation:
    Every decision made through decentralized governance is recorded on the blockchain, ensuring that all actions are visible and verifiable by participants.

8. **Answer: b) They act as voting shares for decision-making.**
    Explanation:
    In decentralized governance, tokens typically represent voting rights. Participants use their tokens to vote on proposals, influencing the organization's direction.

230

CHAPTER 16

A PATH FORWARD FOR FUTURE ENTHUSIASTS AND ERADICATING BAD PLAYERS

Key Points

- Encouraging Responsible Adoption
- Building a Secure and Transparent Ecosystem
- The Role of Technology in Eradicating Illegal Activities
- Collaborative Efforts for a Safer Crypto Space
- The Author's Vision: A Safe and Ethical Crypto World

ENCOURAGING RESPONSIBLE ADOPTION

As blockchain and cryptocurrencies become more integrated into global financial systems, encouraging responsible adoption is crucial for maintaining both the integrity and trust in the space. Education plays a pivotal role here. For new users entering the space, there must be readily available resources that explain the risks and opportunities of blockchain technology. Without a clear understanding of how to engage safely with cryptocurrency, users are more likely to fall victim to scams or make decisions that jeopardize their investments.

Governments and financial institutions are working hard to create an environment where innovation can thrive while also protecting individuals from potential risks. Responsible adoption doesn't just apply to individuals but also to companies. Businesses entering the blockchain ecosystem must ensure that they prioritize transparency, security, and compliance. This includes abiding by Know Your Customer (KYC) and Anti-Money Laundering (AML) regulations, as well as participating in self-regulatory initiatives within the blockchain community.

A major component of responsible adoption is fostering a culture of ethical practices. This means promoting transparency and accountability at all levels of the ecosystem, from individual users to large institutions. Blockchain technology, in its decentralized nature, gives power to the users, but with this comes the responsibility to use that power ethically. Companies and developers in the space are increasingly adopting codes of conduct that promote fairness and discourage predatory behaviors that could harm the ecosystem.

Encouraging responsible adoption also requires a focus on education about security best practices. This is especially important in decentralized finance (DeFi) and other applications where users control their own funds without intermediaries. Teaching users about secure wallet storage, private key management, and understanding how smart contracts work can prevent loss of funds and other security risks.

Lastly, responsible adoption is a global effort. Different countries are at different stages of adoption, and each has its regulatory framework. Cross-border collaboration between governments, financial institutions, and crypto businesses is critical to creating a cohesive framework that encourages responsible adoption while promoting innovation.

BUILDING A SECURE AND TRANSPARENT ECOSYSTEM

A secure and transparent ecosystem is vital for the long-term success of the blockchain and cryptocurrency industries. Trust is the cornerstone of any financial system, and blockchain technology's transparency offers a way to create trust without the need for centralized institutions. Each transaction recorded on a blockchain is immutable, meaning it cannot be altered, which enhances trustworthiness. This transparency helps prevent fraud and provides a clear audit trail for all participants.

Security remains one of the primary concerns for users, investors, and regulators in the blockchain ecosystem. Blockchain networks are vulnerable to hacking, fraud, and other malicious activities if proper precautions aren't taken. As a result, industry players are constantly evolving security protocols and implementing innovative solutions like multi-signature wallets, hardware wallets, and decentralized consensus mechanisms to fortify their platforms. Security audits of smart contracts and decentralized applications (dApps) have also become a standard practice for platforms seeking to establish themselves as reliable.

Building a transparent ecosystem is not just about technology—it's also about accountability. Platforms that handle large amounts of user funds are expected to operate under high standards of transparency. Open-source development and regular audits by third-party organizations help provide assurance to users that their funds and information are safe. In addition, regulators have taken a keen interest in how these platforms operate, leading to the introduction of stricter KYC and AML rules to prevent illegal activities and ensure a secure and transparent financial system.

To foster security and transparency further, collaboration between blockchain companies and regulators is essential. Regulatory bodies play an important role in holding bad actors accountable and ensuring that crypto platforms meet high standards of transparency. Several blockchain companies have embraced this by developing self-regulatory organizations (SROs) to work alongside government agencies, fostering a safer and more transparent environment for both users and businesses.

As blockchain continues to develop, integrating transparency with privacy will remain a delicate balance. Privacy coins and anonymization techniques can offer privacy, but are often criticized for their potential misuse. Developing methods that allow transparent tracking of financial transactions while maintaining user privacy is a challenge that the industry is tackling through cryptographic advancements and privacy-preserving technologies.

THE ROLE OF TECHNOLOGY IN ERADICATING ILLEGAL ACTIVITIES

Technology has always been a double-edged sword, offering the potential for innovation while also being susceptible to misuse. Blockchain technology, despite its benefits, has been exploited by bad actors due to its decentralized and pseudonymous nature. However, advanced blockchain analytics and security tools are making significant progress in eradicating illegal activities by detecting and preventing fraud, money laundering, and other malicious actions within the cryptocurrency space.

Chainalysis

One of the key players in blockchain analytics, **Chainalysis**, partners with government agencies and financial institutions to investigate illicit activities on blockchain networks. Chainalysis uses powerful analytics tools to identify criminal behavior patterns, including money laundering, terrorism financing, and ransomware attacks. Their solutions have been crucial in numerous high-profile investigations, providing actionable insights for law enforcement to trace and seize stolen funds.

Chainalysis also enhances transparency in cryptocurrency markets by providing compliance solutions for exchanges and financial institutions, ensuring adherence to Know Your Customer (KYC) and Anti-Money Laundering (AML) regulations. With their tools, businesses can monitor suspicious transactions, enabling proactive risk management.

Elliptic

Elliptic is another major force in the blockchain analytics space, focusing on fraud prevention and compliance solutions for businesses and institutions. Their real-time risk assessment tools allow for the identification of suspicious transactions, wallets, and addresses before they pose significant issues. By flagging high-risk activities, Elliptic helps companies comply with AML and KYC regulations, which are essential for maintaining secure and transparent financial ecosystems.

Elliptic's platform not only detects fraudulent activities but also provides businesses with data-backed insights, enabling them to mitigate risks while remaining compliant with ever-evolving global regulations.

CipherTrace

CipherTrace provides comprehensive cryptocurrency risk mitigation solutions designed to help exchanges, financial institutions, and governments detect fraud and remain compliant with financial regulations. By offering tools that track transactions across multiple blockchain networks, CipherTrace ensures thorough monitoring and security for users operating in the cryptocurrency space.

Their solutions help users detect illicit transactions, comply with AML and KYC requirements, and ensure their crypto-related operations remain secure. As a leader in blockchain intelligence, CipherTrace is vital in ensuring a safer crypto ecosystem for both businesses and users.

Blockchain Intelligence Group (BIG)

Blockchain Intelligence Group (BIG) has created tools like **QLUE**™, which assist law enforcement agencies in tracing suspicious cryptocurrency transactions. By tracking and analyzing illicit activities in real time, BIG's software allows financial institutions and legal authorities to identify potential illegal behavior more efficiently. This capability helps prevent and resolve crimes such as fraud and money laundering, ensuring that bad actors can be held accountable.

BIG's contributions to compliance and transaction monitoring are instrumental in keeping the cryptocurrency ecosystem safe from illicit actors. Their solutions empower both institutions and governments to uphold the law while fostering a secure environment for users.

TRM Labs and AnChain.AI

TRM Labs and **AnChain.AI** are two key players in the realm of AI-driven blockchain analytics, helping to protect crypto networks from fraud, money laundering, and other illicit activities. **TRM Labs** offers real-time transaction monitoring and threat analysis, providing financial institutions with the tools to identify suspicious activity across multiple blockchains. By using advanced analytics, TRM Labs helps organizations remain compliant with regulations while minimizing their exposure to fraud and criminal activities.

AnChain.AI focuses on integrating AI with blockchain technology to detect suspicious behavior and prevent fraud in decentralized ecosystems. Their machine learning models analyze vast amounts of data to identify patterns of fraud or misuse, safeguarding decentralized applications and exchanges from malicious actors.

Merkle Science

Merkle Science stands out for its predictive blockchain analytics, offering tools that can detect and prevent illegal activities before they occur. By using advanced machine learning algorithms, Merkle Science enables businesses, exchanges, and governments to proactively address threats such as money laundering, fraud, and terrorism financing. Merkle Science's platform identifies suspicious patterns in real-time, providing essential data that helps law enforcement and regulatory agencies intervene before serious damage occurs.

In addition to its focus on fraud detection, Merkle Science helps institutions comply with AML regulations and reduce risks in their crypto operations.

Their innovative approach to predictive analytics has positioned them as a critical player in safeguarding the blockchain ecosystem.

COLLABORATIVE EFFORTS FOR A SAFER CRYPTO SPACE

No single entity can ensure the safety of the entire blockchain space. It takes collaboration between developers, regulators, institutions, and users to create a safer crypto environment. These collaborative efforts are already taking shape in the form of industry-wide initiatives, regulatory frameworks, and partnerships aimed at addressing the security and ethical challenges posed by blockchain technology.

Industry initiatives like the **Blockchain Alliance** bring together blockchain companies, law enforcement, and regulators to promote responsible practices and address illegal activities. Through collaboration and information sharing, the Alliance works to improve the safety and security of the blockchain space. Such initiatives are crucial for creating a unified front against cybercriminals, ensuring that all stakeholders are aligned in the fight against fraud and misuse.

Moreover, platforms are increasingly adopting self-regulatory practices. This involves regular audits of their codebases, continuous monitoring of security threats, and adopting measures that make their platforms more resilient to attacks. Decentralized Autonomous Organizations (DAOs) also play a role in fostering community-driven regulation. DAOs allow communities to vote on security measures and protocol upgrades, ensuring that the ecosystem is governed democratically and in the best interest of all participants.

Global regulatory collaboration is equally important in fostering a safer blockchain ecosystem. Governments worldwide are learning from each other's experiences and working together to create unified guidelines that encourage blockchain innovation while deterring illegal activities. Countries like Malta, Switzerland, and Singapore have developed regulatory frameworks that foster innovation while maintaining high standards of security and compliance.

At the community level, crypto enthusiasts and users are also contributing to security efforts. By sharing knowledge, reporting suspicious activities, and promoting best practices, the blockchain community helps keep the space safer for all participants. Public awareness campaigns and educational initiatives further empower users to engage in the crypto space responsibly.

Finally, collaboration between blockchain developers and financial institutions is helping bridge the gap between decentralized and traditional finance. Financial institutions benefit from blockchain's security and transparency, while blockchain platforms adopt industry standards for fraud detection and regulatory compliance. This partnership ensures that the benefits of blockchain can be realized without compromising security or legal obligations.

THE AUTHOR'S VISION: A SAFE AND ETHICAL CRYPTO WORLD

As we look toward the future, it is undeniable that blockchain technology and cryptocurrency have the power to transform industries, reshape financial systems, and redefine how trust is built in the digital world. This technology holds extraordinary promise, from giving the unbanked access to financial services to creating transparent supply chains and fostering decentralized governance. However, for this potential to be fully realized, it is crucial that the ecosystem remains safe, transparent, and ethical.

The vision for a safe crypto world depends on more than just innovation. It requires continued collaboration between all stakeholders, including developers, entrepreneurs, investors, regulators, and users. It demands a shared commitment to responsible practices, to creating security-first environments, and to preserving the core principles of decentralization and fairness that originally fueled blockchain's rise. As technologies evolve, so must our collective efforts to strengthen security, protect user rights, and maintain the public's trust.

Building a safer and more ethical crypto world is not solely a matter of technical solutions. It is about creating a culture that prioritizes transparency over secrecy, accountability over anonymity, and integrity over short-term gain. True progress comes not just from the code we write, but from the values we embed into the very foundation of this emerging digital economy.

This means encouraging responsible adoption at all levels, from startups launching new tokens to governments crafting regulations. It means fostering collaboration across borders and industries, understanding that no single entity can secure the future of crypto alone. It also means embracing advanced technologies such as artificial intelligence, decentralized identity systems, and stronger encryption that can help detect, deter, and eliminate bad actors without compromising the openness that makes blockchain revolutionary.

The path forward requires commitment not just from developers or regulators but from every participant in the ecosystem. It is a shared responsibility.

- Developers must prioritize security and user protection in their designs.

- Regulators must work to create clear, fair, and innovation-friendly guidelines that protect users without stifling progress.
- Users must educate themselves, practice due diligence, and demand ethical behavior from the platforms and projects they support.

The future of blockchain is not inevitable. It is a future we must choose to build together. By upholding transparency, promoting ethical leadership, and never losing sight of the human impact behind the technology, we can create a blockchain ecosystem that is not only innovative but also sustainable, trustworthy, and inclusive for generations to come.

This is the vision.

This is the opportunity.

This is the responsibility we share.

DEFINITIONS

1. **Blockchain Analytics**: Tools and techniques used to monitor, trace, and analyze blockchain transactions to detect illegal activities and ensure compliance.

2. **Blockchain Intelligence Group (BIG)**: A company specializing in blockchain analytics to track and investigate illegal cryptocurrency transactions for law enforcement and financial institutions.

3. **Know Your Customer (KYC)**: A regulatory process that financial institutions must follow to verify the identity of clients to prevent illegal activities.

4. **Anti-Money Laundering (AML)**: Regulations and procedures that aim to prevent money laundering and other illegal financial activities.

5. **Decentralized Autonomous Organization (DAO)**: A blockchain-based organization governed by smart contracts and community voting, enabling decentralized decision-making.

6. **CipherTrace**: A blockchain analytics company that focuses on detecting fraud and ensuring compliance with KYC/AML regulations

7. **Elliptic**: A company that provides compliance solutions to businesses and financial institutions through blockchain analytics, focusing on preventing money laundering and monitoring suspicious transactions.

8. **Chainalysis**: A blockchain analytics company that tracks cryptocurrency transactions to help detect fraud, money laundering, and terrorism financing, offering tools widely used by government agencies and financial institutions.

9. **TRM Labs**: A blockchain intelligence firm that provides real-time transaction monitoring and risk assessment for fraud, money laundering, and compliance with regulatory frameworks.

10. **AnChain.AI**: A company that focuses on AI-powered blockchain intelligence, using machine learning to secure exchanges and detect fraudulent activity on decentralized platforms.

QUIZ:

Blockchain Security, Compliance, and Governance Tools

1. **What role does Chainalysis play in maintaining a secure blockchain environment?**

    a) It develops decentralized applications (dApps).

    b) It tracks and investigates illegal activities across various blockchain networks.

    c) It builds public blockchains for businesses.

    d) It issues cryptocurrencies.

2. **How does blockchain technology promote transparency?**

    a) By allowing unlimited privacy in transactions.

    b) By making all transaction data publicly available on an immutable ledger.

    c) By using AI to automate all transactions.

    d) By limiting access to transaction records to selected participants.

3. **What is a potential benefit of DAOs in decentralized governance?**

    a) Centralized decision-making.

    b) Complete elimination of governance.

    c) Decentralized voting and automation of rules via smart contracts.

    d) Reduced transparency and accountability.

4. **What function does TRM Labs serve in blockchain ecosystems?**

   a) It creates cryptocurrency exchanges.

   b) It monitors real-time transactions for risks such as fraud and money laundering.

   c) It builds decentralized apps (dApps).

   d) It operates blockchain mining services.

5. **What challenge is posed by the concentration of token ownership in DAOs?**

   a) It increases the number of voters.

   b) It centralizes governance power.

   c) It leads to faster decision-making.

   d) It ensures equal voting power for all participants.

6. **How do technologies like QLUE™ help eradicate illegal activities in the blockchain space?**

   a) By creating new cryptocurrencies.

   b) By providing tracking tools to law enforcement for tracing suspicious cryptocurrency transactions.

   c) By automating cryptocurrency mining.

   d) By restricting blockchain access to certain users.

7. **What is the main focus of Elliptic's blockchain analytics?**

   a) Issuing new blockchain tokens.

   b) Monitoring suspicious transactions and ensuring compliance with AML regulations.

   c) Automating smart contract creation.

   d) Building public blockchain networks.

8. How can Merkle Science's platform aid in the fight against fraud?

   a) By issuing tokens to prevent fraud.

   b) By analyzing transaction patterns to detect suspicious activities early.

   c) By restricting access to blockchains.

   d) By developing new cryptocurrencies.

9. What is the purpose of KYC (Know Your Customer) regulations in the context of blockchain and cryptocurrency?

   a) To prevent identity theft and financial fraud by verifying the identity of users.

   b) To enable anonymous transactions on the blockchain.

   c) To increase transaction fees for exchanges.

   d) To replace AML (Anti-Money Laundering) policies.

☑ ANSWER KEY WITH DETAILED EXPLANATIONS

1. **Answer: b) It tracks and investigates illegal activities across various blockchain networks.**

   Explanation:

   Chainalysis is a leading blockchain analytics firm that helps law enforcement and businesses detect and investigate illicit activities like money laundering and fraud across blockchain networks.

2. **Answer: b) By making all transaction data publicly available on an immutable ledger.**

   Explanation:

   Blockchain technology promotes transparency because transactions are recorded publicly and cannot be altered, ensuring accountability and trust.

3. **Answer: c) Decentralized voting and automation of rules via smart contracts.**

   Explanation:

   DAOs (Decentralized Autonomous Organizations) use blockchain to allow members to vote on decisions transparently, and smart contracts enforce the rules automatically without centralized control.

4. **Answer: b) It monitors real-time transactions for risks such as fraud and money laundering.**

   Explanation:

   TRM Labs provides blockchain intelligence and real-time monitoring services to detect suspicious behavior like money laundering or fraud, helping businesses and regulators maintain compliance.

5. **Answer: b) It centralizes governance power.**
    Explanation:
    If a few individuals or entities hold a large portion of a DAO's tokens, they can dominate decisions, defeating the purpose of decentralization and fairness.

6. **Answer: b) By providing tracking tools to law enforcement for tracing suspicious cryptocurrency transactions.**
    Explanation:
    Technologies like QLUE™ help law enforcement agencies trace and investigate illicit activities on blockchains, supporting efforts to combat fraud, money laundering, and other crimes.

7. **Answer: b) Monitoring suspicious transactions and ensuring compliance with AML regulations.**
    Explanation:
    Elliptic focuses on detecting suspicious blockchain activities and helping institutions comply with Anti-Money Laundering (AML) laws, thereby improving the trust and legitimacy of blockchain operations.

8. **Answer: b) By analyzing transaction patterns to detect suspicious activities early.**
    Explanation:
    Merkle Science uses advanced analytics to spot unusual transaction patterns early, allowing for quicker detection and prevention of fraud and criminal behavior.

9. **Answer: a) To prevent identity theft and financial fraud by verifying the identity of users.**

    Explanation:

    KYC regulations are designed to ensure that crypto users are properly identified, making it harder for bad actors to commit fraud or use cryptocurrencies for illegal purposes.

CHAPTER 17

CONCLUSION:
EMBRACING CHANGE IN THE FINANCIAL WORLD

THE PATH FORWARD FOR EDUCATORS AND LEARNERS

As the financial landscape undergoes transformation through blockchain, decentralized finance (DeFi), and cryptocurrency adoption, it becomes essential for educators and learners to keep pace with these developments. The need for specialized knowledge in cryptography, blockchain infrastructure, and decentralized applications (dApps) is rapidly increasing.

To facilitate the shift, educational institutions must evolve and provide targeted courses that teach not only the technical aspects but also the broader implications of these technologies for industries like finance, supply chains, governance, healthcare, real estate, and entertainment.

Blockchain education is now more accessible than ever, with platforms like Coursera, edX, and Udemy offering a wide range of courses. Specialized certifications, such as the Certified Enterprise Blockchain Professional (CEBP), Certification in Blockchain and Digital Assets (CBDA), and Certified

Blockchain Expert™ (CBE™), are also available to help learners build deeper expertise. There's no one-size-fits-all; you need to find the program that best fits your goals. As blockchain reshapes industries, future professionals in fields like finance, law, computer science, and public policy will need to understand how decentralized technologies work. To meet this demand, universities and technical schools are creating multi-disciplinary programs that blend blockchain fundamentals with ethics, regulatory frameworks, and the broader social impact of financial innovation.

Equally important is the role of lifelong learning. The fast-evolving nature of blockchain, artificial intelligence (AI), and other technological advancements means that professionals must continuously update their skills. Participating in industry webinars, attending conferences such as Consensus or Blockchain Expo, and networking with professionals in the space will be key for individuals looking to stay at the cutting edge of this dynamic field. It's natural to feel overwhelmed at first, but like any revolutionary technology, blockchain becomes easier to understand with consistent study and hands-on exploration.

Lastly, blockchain education must be made inclusive, ensuring people from diverse backgrounds have access to the tools and knowledge needed to engage with this rapidly developing sector. By democratizing education in decentralized finance and blockchain, we can foster a generation of innovators who will lead the next phase of the financial revolution.

FINAL THOUGHTS

Blockchain technology is set to fundamentally reshape financial systems worldwide, challenging traditional banking infrastructure and providing decentralized alternatives that are more transparent, accessible, and inclusive. However, this technological transformation will not come without its challenges, particularly in terms of regulatory alignment, ethical governance, and the widespread integration of blockchain into everyday life.

Financial systems have historically evolved gradually, but the pace of technological change, driven by blockchain and cryptocurrency, is accelerating this evolution faster than ever. The emergence of decentralized finance platforms, digital identities, and tokenized assets signals the beginning of a new financial era. Still, these advancements must be accompanied by robust regulatory frameworks and international cooperation to prevent misuse, fraud, and illegal activity.

As we look ahead, the role of individuals and organizations alike will be crucial in building a more secure and transparent ecosystem. Developers, financial institutions, and regulators must work collaboratively to integrate blockchain technology without compromising the security and trust of the financial system.

Adopting blockchain is not just about technology; it requires a shift in mindset. The path forward involves rethinking how economies operate, reimagining governance systems, and embracing decentralized networks' possibilities. As we continue to build this future, all stakeholders must take a responsible and ethical approach to ensure a secure, transparent, and inclusive financial world.

CALL TO ACTION

The journey toward a decentralized future starts with you. Whether you're an educator, student, developer, or business leader, you have a role in shaping the next phase of the global financial system. Start by educating yourself, understanding the key concepts of blockchain, and exploring the practical applications of these technologies.

Join blockchain communities, engage in conversations with thought leaders, and explore decentralized applications. Developers can start building, while financial institutions can begin exploring pilot projects to integrate blockchain solutions into their operations. Regulators must actively collaborate with industry players to foster innovation while ensuring that these technologies comply with global financial laws and standards.

A decentralized financial world is within reach. It promises greater financial inclusion, reduced transaction costs, and a more transparent system. But we must build it responsibly. Take the first step by diving into blockchain's potential, embracing new ways of thinking, and contributing to an ecosystem that supports innovation without compromising on trust or security.

QUOTE

"Change is the law of life. And those who look only to the past or present are certain to miss the future."

– John F. Kennedy

This quote reflects the importance of embracing new technologies, like blockchain, to ensure that we are not left behind in the evolving financial world.

QUIZ: CHAPTER 17

Conclusion: Embracing Change in the Financial World

1. How can educators prepare students for the rapidly evolving financial landscape driven by blockchain technology?

   a) By focusing only on traditional finance principles

   b) By incorporating blockchain and decentralized finance into curricula

   c) By discouraging the use of cryptocurrency

   d) By promoting only physical currency transactions

2. Why is lifelong learning crucial in the blockchain and cryptocurrency space?

   a) Because traditional finance is not evolving

   b) Because blockchain and crypto technologies evolve rapidly, requiring continuous updates to knowledge and skills

   c) Because online courses are available

   d) Because it is mandated by financial regulations

3. What role do regulatory frameworks play in the adoption of blockchain technologies?

   a) They hinder the growth of blockchain technology

   b) They facilitate the widespread use of blockchain while ensuring compliance with laws

   c) They focus only on cryptocurrencies

   d) They are not necessary for decentralized technologies

4. **Which of the following is a benefit of blockchain technology in financial systems?**

    a) Increased transparency and reduced transaction costs

    b) Decreased transparency but faster transactions

    c) Increased reliance on central authorities

    d) Slower transaction processing

5. **What is the significance of decentralized finance (DeFi)?**

    a) It centralizes control of financial systems

    b) It eliminates intermediaries and enables peer-to-peer financial transactions

    c) It uses physical currencies for transactions

    d) It operates solely within centralized banks

6. **Why is blockchain technology seen as a democratizing force in finance?**

    a) It centralizes control over money

    b) It offers access to financial services for underserved populations

    c) It is restricted to wealthier individuals

    d) It increases transaction fees

7. **How can blockchain ensure financial security while providing transparency?**

    a) By encrypting all transactions and making them immutable

    b) By centralizing all transactions under one authority

    c) By allowing only verified institutions to use the blockchain

    d) By keeping transactions private and unrecorded

8. **What is the significance of tokenized assets in the future of finance?**

   a) They represent physical ownership of assets that can be traded digitally on blockchain networks

   b) They eliminate the need for any physical currency

   c) They increase transaction fees for physical assets

   d) They make traditional assets obsolete

9. **What challenge is associated with blockchain technology that still needs addressing?**

   a) Increased transaction speed

   b) Scalability and regulatory alignment

   c) The use of fiat currencies

   d) The dependence on physical banks

10. **Which of the following is essential for embracing blockchain in education?**

    a) Avoiding decentralized technologies

    b) Developing multi-disciplinary programs that cover both technical and ethical aspects

    c) Focusing on traditional finance only

    d) Limiting access to blockchain education

☑ ANSWER KEY WITH DETAILED EXPLANATIONS

1. **b) By incorporating blockchain and decentralized finance into curricula**

   Explanation:

   The chapter stresses that educators must update their curricula to include blockchain and DeFi concepts, preparing students for the decentralized financial world instead of only teaching traditional banking.

2. **b) Because blockchain and crypto technologies evolve rapidly, requiring continuous updates to knowledge and skills**

   Explanation:

   Blockchain and cryptocurrency are fast-moving fields. Lifelong learning—through courses, webinars, and networking—is crucial to stay up to date with new developments.

3. **b) They facilitate the widespread use of blockchain while ensuring compliance with laws**

   Explanation:

   Regulations help legitimize blockchain, making it safer for users and investors. Good regulatory frameworks promote innovation while protecting the financial system.

4. **a) Increased transparency and reduced transaction costs**

   Explanation:

   Blockchain creates permanent, public records of transactions and eliminates many traditional fees associated with middlemen, as emphasized throughout the chapter.

5. **b) It eliminates intermediaries and enables peer-to-peer financial transactions**

    Explanation:

    DeFi platforms allow users to lend, borrow, and trade without traditional banks or brokers, creating faster, more direct financial interactions.

6. **b) It offers access to financial services for underserved populations**

    Explanation:

    Blockchain opens up financial services to millions of people who have no access to traditional banking, helping to democratize finance globally.

7. **a) By encrypting all transactions and making them immutable**

    Explanation:

    Blockchain's security comes from encryption and immutability, meaning transactions cannot be changed after being recorded, ensuring both security and transparency.

8. **a) They represent physical ownership of assets that can be traded digitally on blockchain networks**

    Explanation:

    Tokenized assets convert real-world items (like real estate or art) into digital form, allowing easier, faster, and safer trading on blockchain systems.

9. **b) Scalability and regulatory alignment**

    Explanation:

    The chapter notes that two major hurdles for blockchain adoption are improving transaction capacity (scalability) and harmonizing laws across countries (regulatory alignment).

10. **b) Developing multi-disciplinary programs that cover both technical and ethical aspects**

   Explanation:

   Future education must be broad—not just technical. Schools must also teach ethical considerations, legal frameworks, and the broader societal impacts of blockchain.

CHAPTER 18

EXPERT INTERVIEWS

Key Points

- Interviews with Thought Leaders
- Insights from Developers
- Perspectives from Investors
- Key Figures in the Blockchain Industry
- The Future of Blockchain According to Experts

INTERVIEWS WITH THOUGHT LEADERS

In the blockchain and cryptocurrency space, thought leaders play a pivotal role in shaping narratives, driving innovation, and influencing regulatory and industry trends. Their insights help us understand the deeper forces pushing blockchain technology forward — and the hurdles it must overcome to achieve widespread adoption.

Vitalik Buterin, co-founder of Ethereum, remains one of the most influential figures in blockchain. His vision for decentralized applications (dApps) and smart contracts has helped redefine what blockchain can achieve beyond simple financial transactions. Following Ethereum's successful transition to Proof-of-Stake (known as "The Merge") in 2022, Buterin has emphasized the urgent need for scalability through innovations like sharding and rollups. In recent interviews, Buterin stresses that the future of blockchain hinges on the technology's ability to support a decentralized world where finance, governance, and identity are democratized and accessible globally.

Andreas Antonopoulos, a powerful voice for Bitcoin and decentralized systems, remains a steadfast advocate for individual financial sovereignty. His talks highlight the technical advantages of blockchain and the profound ethical and philosophical implications: empowering individuals against oppressive or inefficient centralized systems. Antonopoulos emphasizes that true decentralization comes with responsibilities, such as education, security practices, and self-custody, that must be embraced if blockchain is to fulfill its potential.

Meltem Demirors, Chief Strategy Officer at CoinShares, offers a broader societal lens. She often speaks about blockchain's capacity to reshape power structures far beyond finance, impacting art, media, culture, and governance. Demirors warns that as blockchain technology becomes more mainstream, it faces risks of being "captured" or co-opted by the very institutions it seeks to disrupt. Her message urges vigilance: to ensure that decentralization remains authentic, not merely a buzzword used by corporations.

Adding to these insights, Balaji Srinivasan has advocated for "network states" — digital communities organized online but having real-world impact. His vision suggests blockchain will be foundational not just in business or tech, but in building new societal models altogether.

INSIGHTS FROM DEVELOPERS

Behind every blockchain breakthrough are developers, the people who build the protocols, scale the networks, and solve the engineering problems no one else sees.

Nick Szabo, credited with conceptualizing smart contracts, remains a guiding light for the developer community. He continues to emphasize the critical importance of cryptographic security and minimizing reliance on human intermediaries. In his view, blockchain's real revolution is the creation of trustless systems — frameworks where agreements and transactions happen without needing to "trust" third parties, thereby reducing corruption, fraud, and inefficiency.

Developers at Chainlink highlight the growing importance of decentralized oracles — systems that connect blockchain smart contracts with real-world data. Oracles power many DeFi products, insurance applications, and even gaming ecosystems. More recently, Chainlink's Cross-Chain Interoperability Protocol (CCIP) has been working to bridge different blockchains, tackling one of blockchain's biggest hurdles: fragmentation.

Ethereum developers, after The Merge, now turn their attention to scalability improvements. Projects like Danksharding and EIP-4844 (proto-danksharding) seek to make Ethereum transactions cheaper and faster without compromising decentralization. Their work reflects the new era of blockchain innovation: solving for global usability without sacrificing the founding ideals of transparency and user empowerment.

Emerging Layer 2 solutions, like Optimism, Arbitrum, and Base (Coinbase's Layer 2 network), are providing developers with faster, cheaper environments to build on, while maintaining Ethereum's security. Leaders like Jesse Pollak (Coinbase) and Ryan Wyatt (Polygon Labs) have voiced that the next phase of Web3 will be user-centric, making blockchain "invisible" to users while offering its benefits underneath the surface.

Anatoly Yakovenko, founder of Solana, continues to advocate for a future where blockchain transactions happen at web speeds, enabling real-time gaming, payments, and applications on-chain. Although Solana has faced technical setbacks, its commitment to fast, scalable blockchain networks represents an important alternative vision to Ethereum's slower but more decentralized model.

PERSPECTIVES FROM INVESTORS

Investors not only provide capital, they shape trends, reward innovations, and often set the narrative about where the future is headed. As blockchain continues to evolve from a niche technology into a global infrastructure, the insights of investors reveal where the momentum — and the money — are flowing.

Chamath Palihapitiya, venture capitalist and early Bitcoin advocate, remains bullish on Bitcoin's role as a digital equivalent of gold. In his view, Bitcoin's decentralized structure and finite supply make it a hedge against inflation, systemic collapse, and state overreach. Palihapitiya often stresses the importance of diversification, suggesting that crypto should be a part — but not the entirety — of a thoughtful, risk-managed investment portfolio.

Cathy Wood, founder of ARK Invest, consistently emphasizes blockchain's convergence with other disruptive technologies such as artificial intelligence, robotics, energy storage, and genomics. Wood envisions blockchain serving as the financial backbone of a machine-driven economy, where autonomous organizations and decentralized data markets reshape industries. Her belief that blockchain will underpin new AI-native applications highlights the growing synergy between these once-separate technological frontiers.

Balaji Srinivasan, former CTO of Coinbase and an influential investor, offers a slightly different angle. He has heavily backed decentralized autonomous organizations (DAOs), privacy technologies, and decentralized finance (DeFi) protocols. Srinivasan argues that crypto is not just a new investment class, it's an existential toolkit for individuals looking to exit broken institutions and build self-sovereign communities. His advocacy for "network states" reflects a belief that blockchain will power entirely new forms of governance and societal structure.

Beyond individual investors, **institutional investors are entering the space more cautiously but no less significantly**. Major asset managers like **BlackRock, Fidelity**, and **Invesco** have begun offering crypto exposure to clients through Bitcoin ETFs, crypto-backed funds, and blockchain-related equities. While these moves signal growing mainstream acceptance, critics warn that the influx of institutional money could dilute the original decentralized ethos that fueled early blockchain development.

The entry of heavyweight venture capital firms has further transformed the blockchain investment landscape.

Andreessen Horowitz (a16z Crypto), led by Marc Andreessen and Chris Dixon, is one of the most prominent and aggressive investors in blockchain and Web3 technology. With billions committed through dedicated crypto funds, a16z backs projects in decentralized finance, NFTs, gaming, social media, and Layer 1 blockchains. Their belief that blockchain represents the next great computing platform, the foundation of "Web3" has helped drive broader awareness and innovation across the tech world.

Digital Currency Group (DCG), founded by Barry Silbert, acts as an influential parent company across the blockchain space, controlling stakes in **Grayscale Investments** (the world's largest digital asset manager), **Foundry** (a leading mining services company), and formerly **Genesis** (a major crypto lending platform). Through a web of interconnected investments, DCG plays a quiet but powerful role in setting the pace and direction of blockchain's institutional evolution.

Michael Saylor, Executive Chairman of **MicroStrategy**, became one of the most visible Bitcoin proponents after allocating billions of company dollars into Bitcoin reserves. Saylor frames Bitcoin not just as an investment but as "digital property," a superior, incorruptible form of wealth storage compared to traditional fiat currencies. His high-profile advocacy helped usher in a wave of corporate Bitcoin treasury strategies during the 2020–2022 bull market.

Pantera Capital, founded by Dan Morehead, stands out as one of the earliest crypto-focused investment firms. Pantera's diverse portfolio spans DeFi, blockchain infrastructure, NFT platforms, and tokenization projects. Their forward-leaning investment thesis argues that blockchain technology will revolutionize financial systems, supply chains, gaming, and identity management at a global scale.

Even traditional giants like **Sequoia Capital** have entered the blockchain space. Though famously burned by investments like **FTX**, Sequoia remains committed to backing blockchain and Web3 ventures, particularly in infrastructure, cybersecurity, decentralized applications, and the integration of AI with blockchain technologies.

Adding to this dynamic landscape, newer hybrid funds such as **Multicoin Capital**, **Paradigm**, and **Framework Ventures** focus exclusively on crypto-native projects — betting on decentralized governance models, Web3 gaming, decentralized social networks, and emerging Layer 2 scalability solutions.

While the influx of venture capital and institutional money brings credibility, resources, and broader reach, it also raises fundamental questions:

Can blockchain maintain its decentralization principles under the weight of traditional finance?
Will innovation be driven by open communities or shaped by corporate interests?

And how will regulators adapt to this fast-moving fusion of finance and technology?

As investors continue to shape blockchain's trajectory, it remains clear that the future will be a delicate balancing act — between decentralization and scalability, innovation and regulation, opportunity and risk.

KEY FIGURES IN THE BLOCKCHAIN INDUSTRY

Beyond investors and developers, certain individuals have become synonymous with blockchain's growth and global reach.

Changpeng Zhao (CZ), founder and former CEO of Binance, remains one of the most influential figures in cryptocurrency's expansion to mainstream audiences. His leadership, though not without controversy, helped propel Binance to the world's largest crypto exchange by volume. Even after stepping down in 2023, CZ's vision of fast, accessible, low-cost crypto access continues through projects like Binance Smart Chain and the broader Binance ecosystem.

Joseph Lubin, co-founder of Ethereum and founder of ConsenSys, has spent the past decade advancing the Ethereum ecosystem. His work in promoting Web3 — the decentralized internet — positions him at the center of efforts to replace today's centralized digital economy with user-owned networks and decentralized applications.

Elizabeth Stark, CEO of Lightning Labs, is tackling Bitcoin's scalability problem head-on through Layer 2 solutions like the Lightning Network. Her vision is for Bitcoin to be used not only as a store of value but also as a practical, everyday payment system — achieving both security and speed.

Vitalik Buterin, though often categorized with developers, also acts as a philosopher-king of blockchain thought. His ideas about decentralized identity, voting, and governance shape much of Ethereum's research direction, and increasingly influence global blockchain standards.

Emerging figures like Stani Kulechov (Aave/ Lens Protocol) are pushing blockchain into new territories, including decentralized social media — challenging giants like Twitter and Facebook with Web3-native alternatives.

THE FUTURE OF BLOCKCHAIN ACCORDING TO EXPERTS

Despite different specializations and philosophies, one thing is clear: blockchain is no longer a speculative technology. It's a foundational infrastructure being actively built into the future economy, society, and governance.

Vitalik Buterin sees blockchain becoming the invisible layer that underpins digital identity, decentralized finance, global governance, and collaborative digital organizations.

Meltem Demirors predicts a power shift, where traditional gatekeepers (banks, governments, corporations) must contend with decentralized alternatives that offer greater transparency, accountability, and user control.

Developers predict the rise of "modular blockchains" — where chains like Ethereum, Celestia, and others specialize in different layers (data availability, consensus, execution) but interoperate seamlessly. They foresee decentralized social media, gaming economies, and even health data networks becoming normal parts of daily life.

Investors like Cathy Wood and Balaji Srinivasan argue that blockchain will become to finance and governance what the internet became to communication — a fundamental revolution that spawns new industries, disrupts legacy structures, and offers individuals more agency over their money, identity, and voice.

However, experts warn that blockchain's future depends heavily on how regulatory battles unfold, how effectively projects scale without sacrificing security, and whether the ethos of decentralization survives the tidal wave of corporate and institutional adoption.

The journey ahead will be shaped not only by technology, but by the values, governance models, and community choices made along the way.

🗐 CONCLUSION

If there is one thing this chapter shows, it is that blockchain is not just about technology anymore. It is about people. The thinkers, the builders, the investors, the dreamers, and the leaders who are shaping what this whole space could become.

Thought leaders like Vitalik Buterin, Andreas Antonopoulos, and Meltem Demirors are not just giving talks at conferences or writing papers. They are putting forward real ideas that challenge the way we think about trust, ownership, and control. They are showing us that blockchain is not just a better way to move money around. It is a better way to move value, ideas, identity, and power across the world. They see a future where systems are not just open to a few but open to everyone. A world where you do not have to trust a government or a corporation blindly, because you can verify everything yourself.

Developers, who often do not get the headlines or the recognition, are solving the hard problems that make this future possible. Thanks to them, we have already seen huge steps forward. Ethereum completed its shift to Proof of Stake, slashing its energy use and setting a new standard for blockchain sustainability. Chainlink built the bridges that connect blockchains to real world data like stock prices, weather reports, and election results. Layer 2 networks like Optimism and Arbitrum are scaling Ethereum so it can support millions of users without sky high fees. These developers are not just coding. They are building the future one breakthrough at a time.

Investors have played a powerful role too. Chamath Palihapitiya, Cathy Wood, Balaji Srinivasan, and entire firms like Andreessen Horowitz and Digital Currency Group have shown the world that blockchain is not just a playground for speculators. It is an ecosystem for real innovation. Their investments are helping fund the next generation of ideas, from decentralized finance to decentralized identity, gaming, healthcare, and beyond. They are betting on a future where users, not middlemen, control the value they create.

Key figures like Changpeng Zhao, Joseph Lubin, Elizabeth Stark, and others are in the trenches, building the companies and platforms that bring blockchain to life for everyday people. They are tackling challenges like regulatory uncertainty, cybersecurity threats, and scaling headaches. They are doing the real work of turning blockchain from an idea into something you can use with your phone, your computer, or even your car. Without them, blockchain would stay locked inside whitepapers and tech circles. Because of them, it is breaking into the real world, bit by bit.

One of the most exciting parts of all of this is how unpredictable it is. No single person, company, or country controls blockchain. It is being shaped by thousands of projects, millions of contributors, and billions of ideas. It is messy. It is chaotic. And that is exactly what gives it so much creative energy.

We are already seeing early signs of what is possible. Bitcoin proved that you could have money without a central bank. Ethereum proved that you could have contracts without needing lawyers or courts in the middle. Projects like Uniswap and Aave are showing that you can have lending, borrowing, and trading without giant financial institutions standing between you and your money. DAOs are proving that you can have organizations without CEOs or centralized boards. Decentralized identity tools are beginning to show that you can prove who you are without handing over all your private data.

But with all this potential comes real challenges. Blockchain still faces major hurdles. It needs to scale faster, handle more users, and cut down energy usage even more. It needs to become easier for everyday people to use without needing a degree in computer science. It needs clear, fair regulations that protect users without choking off innovation. It needs to stay true to its values of decentralization and user empowerment, even as big corporations and Wall Street start showing up with deep pockets and strong influence.

Because the truth is, blockchain could change everything for the better. But if we are not careful, it could also end up repeating the same problems it was meant to solve.

That is why what happens now matters so much.

The values we choose.

The projects we support.

The leaders we follow.

The decisions we make today will shape the blockchain future for generations.

The good news is, we are not powerless. We are not spectators.

We are part of the story.

Every builder, every investor, every educator, every learner, every skeptic asking good questions, every believer pushing for better systems, all of us are part of writing what comes next.

Blockchain is not just about technology anymore. It is about community. It is about creativity. It is about courage.

It is about believing that a better future is possible and being willing to help build it.

❄ FINAL REFLECTION

At its heart, blockchain is not just code, charts, coins, or passwords on a screen. It is an idea—a bold, messy, powerful idea that says maybe, just maybe, we can do things differently.

Maybe we can build systems that are not designed to trap people but to empower them.

Maybe we can build economies where gatekeepers do not siphon your value before it reaches you.

Maybe we can build communities that are not controlled by a few at the top but guided by the many who participate.

This will not be easy. Change never is.

There will be hacks, scandals, losses, and hard lessons.

There will be moments when people lose hope, when it feels easier to slide back into the old ways of doing things.

There will be real forces fighting to keep the status quo alive.

But every time a developer fixes a bug, or an investor backs a bold new idea, or a young person downloads their first crypto wallet and takes control of their own money, the world shifts a little closer to something better.

Every small step matters.

Every conversation matters.

Every block added to the chain matters.

You do not have to be a billionaire or a tech genius to make a difference. You must care enough to learn, to ask good questions, to share ideas, and to dream about what is possible.

Because at the end of the day, the real power of blockchain is not just in the technology.

It is in the people who believe that open systems, open communities, and open futures are worth building and protecting.

The story of blockchain is still being written.

And you, whether you are reading this book, investing in your first token, building your first app, or simply trying to understand how it all works, you are already part of it.

The future of blockchain is wide open.

And it belongs to all of us.

ADDITIONAL INFORMATION:

This section serves as a comprehensive reference for readers, compiling essential terminology, resources for further education, and a robust set of frequently asked questions. By providing this information, we aim to enhance your understanding of blockchain and cryptocurrency.

Glossary of Terms

1. **Altcoin:** Any cryptocurrency other than Bitcoin, including Ethereum, Litecoin, and Ripple.
2. **Bitcoin:** The first and most widely recognized cryptocurrency, created by an anonymous entity known as Satoshi Nakamoto in 2009.
3. **Blockchain:** A decentralized digital ledger that records transactions across a network of computers, ensuring security and immutability.
4. **Central Bank Digital Currency (CBDC):** A digital form of fiat currency issued and regulated by a country's central bank.
5. **Cold Storage:** The practice of storing cryptocurrencies offline to protect them from hacking.
6. **Cryptocurrency:** Digital or virtual currency that uses cryptography for security, operating independently of a central bank.
7. **Cryptography:** The practice of securing information by transforming it into an unreadable format, requiring a key for decryption.
8. **Decentralization:** The process of distributing power and control away from a central authority or institution.
9. **Digital Wallet:** An electronic device or software that allows an individual to make electronic transactions, such as holding digital currencies like CBDCs.
10. **Distributed Ledger Technology (DLT):** The technology underlying blockchain, where data is shared and synchronized across multiple locations without a central authority.

11. **DAO (Decentralized Autonomous Organization):** An organization governed by smart contracts on a blockchain, where decisions are made through decentralized voting by stakeholders.

12. **DeFi (Decentralized Finance):** Financial services offered on a decentralized blockchain network without the need for intermediaries like banks.

13. **Gas Fee:** A fee paid to miners to process transactions and execute smart contracts on the Ethereum network.

14. **Halving:** A process by which the reward for mining Bitcoin transactions is cut in half, occurring approximately every four years.

15. **Hash Function:** A mathematical function that converts an input into a fixed-length string of characters, often used in blockchain to secure data.

16. **Hot Storage:** The practice of storing cryptocurrencies in online wallets that are connected to the internet, making them more accessible but more vulnerable to hacks.

17. **Interoperability:** The ability of different blockchain networks to communicate and share data with one another.

18. **Liquidity Pool:** A collection of funds locked into a smart contract to facilitate trading on decentralized exchanges.

19. **Mining:** The process of validating blockchain transactions and adding them to the distributed ledger by solving complex mathematical problems.

20. **Multi-Signature Wallet:** A type of wallet that requires multiple private keys to authorize a transaction, adding an extra layer of security.

21. **NFT (Non-Fungible Token):** A type of digital asset that represents ownership of a unique item or piece of content, stored on a blockchain.

22. **Oracles:** External data sources that feed real-world information into a blockchain to enable the execution of smart contracts.

23. **Proof of Stake (PoS):** A consensus mechanism where participants are selected to validate transactions based on the number of coins they hold and are willing to "stake" as collateral.

24. **Proof of Work (PoW):** A consensus mechanism in which participants (miners) solve computational puzzles to validate transactions and add them to the blockchain.

25. **Quadratic Voting:** A voting mechanism that allows participants to express the strength of their preferences rather than just a binary yes/no choice.

26. **Regulatory Sandbox:** A framework that allows for live testing of new technologies in a controlled environment under a regulator's supervision.

27. **Sharding:** A process in which blockchain data is split into smaller parts (shards) to improve scalability and transaction processing speed.

28. **Smart Contract:** A self-executing contract where the terms of the agreement are directly written into code on the blockchain.

29. **Stablecoin:** A type of cryptocurrency pegged to a stable asset such as fiat currency to minimize price volatility.

30. **Tokenization:** The process of converting ownership rights or assets into digital tokens that can be traded on a blockchain.

31. **Yield Farming:** The practice of lending or staking cryptocurrency in exchange for rewards, usually in the form of interest or additional tokens.

RESOURCES FOR FURTHER LEARNING:

To expand your knowledge of blockchain and cryptocurrency, consider exploring the following resources:

1. Books:

- *Mastering Bitcoin* by Andreas Antonopoulos
  A comprehensive guide to Bitcoin, blockchain, and cryptocurrency, suitable for both beginners and experts.

- *The Bitcoin Standard* by Saifedean Ammous
  An exploration of Bitcoin's economic principles and its potential to disrupt traditional financial systems.

- *Mastering Ethereum* by Andreas Antonopoulos and Gavin Wood
  An in-depth technical guide to Ethereum, covering everything from the basics to advanced concepts in smart contracts.

- *Blockchain Basics: A Non-Technical Introduction in 25 Steps* by Daniel Drescher
  A straightforward introduction to blockchain technology that breaks down complex concepts into digestible steps.

- *Cryptoassets: The Innovative Investor's Guide to Bitcoin and Beyond* by Chris Burniske and Jack Tatar
  An essential guide for understanding crypto assets, investment strategies, and the broader crypto market landscape.

- *Blockchain Revolution* by Don Tapscott and Alex Tapscott
  An insightful exploration of how blockchain technology is changing the world, from business to government.

- *The Basics of Bitcoins and Blockchains* by Antony Lewis
  A beginner-friendly guide that covers the fundamentals of Bitcoin, blockchain, and cryptocurrencies.
- *The Truth About Crypto: A Practical Guide to Bitcoin, Blockchain, and Beyond by* Ric Edelman
  This book demystifies the world of cryptocurrency, providing clear explanations and practical advice for navigating the crypto landscape.

2. Online Courses:

- **Coursera:**
  - "Bitcoin and Cryptocurrency Technologies"
  - "Blockchain Basics"
  - "Decentralized Finance (DeFi): The Future of Finance"
  - "Smart Contracts"
  - "Blockchain Specialization" by the University of Buffalo
- **Udemy:**
  - "Blockchain for Beginners"
  - "Ethereum and Solidity: The Complete Developer's Guide."
  - "The Complete Cryptocurrency Course: More than 5 Courses in 1."
  - "Cryptocurrency Trading: Complete Guide on How to Trade Crypto."
  - "NFTs: The Complete Guide to Non-Fungible Tokens"
- **edX:**
  - "Blockchain for Business."
  - "Introduction to Hyperledger Blockchain Technologies."

- o "FinTech: Foundations & Applications of Financial Technology."
  - o "Blockchain Fundamentals" by UC Berkeley.
  - o "Blockchain in Business" by The Linux Foundation
- LinkedIn Learning:
  - o *Learning Bitcoin and Other Cryptocurrencies* (Instructor: Tom Geller)
  - o *Blockchain Basics* (Instructor: Jonathan Reichental)
  - o *Blockchain: Learning Solidity* – covering the fundamentals of smart contract development
  - o *Build an Ethereum Blockchain App* – a comprehensive learning path focused on Ethereum tools, dApp development, and smart contract creation

3. Websites & Blogs:

- **CoinDesk** (www.coindesk.com)
  A leading news platform for cryptocurrency and blockchain industry updates.

- **CoinTelegraph** (www.cointelegraph.com)
  Provides news, analysis, and insights on the blockchain and cryptocurrency space.

- **Medium's Cryptocurrency Blogs**
  A platform where numerous authors and experts share thoughts and analyses on various blockchain-related topics.

- **The Block** (www.theblock.co)
  Offers in-depth analysis, research, and news about blockchain technology and cryptocurrency markets.

- **Decrypt** (www.decrypt.co)
  A news site covering the intersection of blockchain and cryptocurrency, focusing on user-friendly content.

- **CryptoSlate** (www.cryptoslate.com)
  A comprehensive source for cryptocurrency news, data, and research, featuring a detailed directory of coins and blockchain companies.

- **Messari** (www.messari.io)
  Provides crypto news, analysis, and research tools to help investors make informed decisions.

- **CoinGecko** (www.coingecko.com)
  An extensive platform for tracking cryptocurrency prices, market capitalization, and analytics.

- **Token Metrics** (www.tokenmetrics.com)
  Offers AI-driven cryptocurrency research and investment insights, focusing on market trends and asset evaluation.

- **Hackernoon** (www.hackernoon.com)
  A technology-focused publication that covers a range of topics, including blockchain, cryptocurrency, and software development.

4. YouTube Channels:

- **Andreas Antonopoulos**
  Renowned for his clear explanations of Bitcoin, blockchain technology, and decentralized systems.

- **Ivan on Tech**
  Covers educational content on cryptocurrency and blockchain development, aimed at both beginners and experienced users.

- **Coin Bureau**

  Provides in-depth reviews and insights into various blockchain projects and market trends.

- **DataDash**

  Offers market analysis, cryptocurrency news, and insights into investment strategies.

- **Lark Davis (The Crypto Lark)**

  Focuses on cryptocurrency trends, investment strategies, and news updates, making complex topics more accessible.

- **Crypto Bobby**

  Provides insights into cryptocurrency trading, investing, and the latest market news.

- **BitBoy Crypto**

  Offers daily news, price analysis, and educational content on various cryptocurrencies and blockchain developments.

- **Crypto Zombie**

  Features animated content explaining blockchain concepts, crypto news, and market updates in an engaging format.

- **Finematics**

  Explains DeFi and crypto concepts with detailed animations, making complex ideas easier to understand.

- **The Modern Investor**

  Focuses on cryptocurrency investment strategies, market trends, and news updates relevant to investors.

- **CryptoStache**

  Provides tutorials, reviews, and insights on various blockchain projects, with a focus on NFT culture.

5. Podcasts:

- **Unchained** hosted by Laura Shin

  A podcast focusing on the people and ideas in blockchain and cryptocurrency, featuring interviews with industry leaders.

- **The Bad Crypto Podcast**

  A fun and informative podcast that covers the latest news in the cryptocurrency world with a light-hearted approach.

- **The Pomp Podcast** hosted by Anthony Pompliano

  Discusses the intersection of finance, business, and cryptocurrency with industry leaders, exploring investment strategies and market trends.

- **Epicenter**

  A podcast that interviews developers, entrepreneurs, and researchers in the blockchain and cryptocurrency space, providing deep insights into projects and technologies.

- **What Bitcoin Did** hosted by Peter McCormack

  Covers a wide range of topics related to Bitcoin, cryptocurrency, and the blockchain industry through expert interviews and discussions.

- **Crypto 101**

  A podcast aimed at newcomers to the cryptocurrency space, providing foundational knowledge and insights on various topics.

- **The Chopping Block**

  Features discussions on current events in cryptocurrency, industry analysis, and interviews with key figures in the space.

- **The Decrypt Daily**

  A podcast that provides daily updates on cryptocurrency news, market analysis, and interviews with experts.

- **CoinTalk**

  A podcast that covers various topics in the cryptocurrency space, including market trends, project deep dives, and interviews with industry professionals.

FREQUENTLY ASKED QUESTIONS (FAQS)

Q1: What is the difference between Bitcoin and Ethereum?

Bitcoin is primarily a digital currency designed for peer-to-peer transactions, while Ethereum is a platform for decentralized applications (dApps) that supports smart contracts, enabling more complex functionalities.

Q2: How do I store cryptocurrency safely?

Cryptocurrency can be stored in wallets, which can be either hardware (offline, more secure) or software (online, more convenient). It's essential to keep your private keys secure, as they control access to your funds.

Q3: What is a blockchain?

A blockchain is a decentralized ledger that records transactions across a network of computers, ensuring transparency, security, and immutability through consensus mechanisms like Proof of Work (PoW) or Proof of Stake (PoS).

Q4: How does mining work?

Mining involves using computational power to validate transactions and add them to the blockchain. Miners solve complex mathematical problems and, upon solving them, earn cryptocurrency as a reward.

Q5: What are gas fees, and why can they be high?

Gas fees are transaction costs on blockchain networks, paid to miners for processing transactions. Fees can rise during times of high demand when more users are trying to execute transactions simultaneously.

Q6: What are the risks associated with investing in cryptocurrency?

Cryptocurrency investments carry risks such as price volatility, regulatory uncertainty, cybersecurity threats, and the potential loss of access due to lost private keys. It's crucial to conduct thorough research and consider long-term strategies.

Q7: What is the significance of smart contracts?

Smart contracts are self-executing agreements coded on the blockchain that automatically enforce and execute terms without intermediaries, which reduces the risk of fraud and enhances trust in transactions.

Q8: How can I get involved in blockchain development?

To become a blockchain developer, start by learning programming languages relevant to blockchain (e.g., Solidity for Ethereum), participate in open-source projects, and take online courses that provide practical experience in blockchain technologies.

Q9: What are stablecoins, and how do they work?

Stablecoins are cryptocurrencies designed to maintain a stable value by pegging them to a reserve of assets, typically fiat currency. This minimizes price volatility and makes them more suitable for transactions.

Q10: What is the role of oracles in blockchain?

Oracles are third-party services that provide external data to blockchain networks, enabling smart contracts to execute based on real-world information, such as price feeds or weather data.

Q11: What is yield farming?

Yield farming is a practice in decentralized finance (DeFi) where users lend or stake their cryptocurrency to earn interest or rewards, often in the form of additional tokens.

Q12: How do decentralized exchanges work?

Decentralized exchanges (DEXs) allow users to trade cryptocurrencies directly with one another without relying on a centralized intermediary. They use smart contracts to facilitate transactions and maintain liquidity.

Q13: What is the purpose of a liquidity pool?

A liquidity pool is a collection of funds locked into a smart contract that facilitates trading on decentralized exchanges. It provides liquidity for trading pairs, allowing users to buy and sell assets more efficiently.

Q14: What is the difference between hot and cold storage?

Hot storage refers to storing cryptocurrencies in online wallets that are connected to the internet, making them more accessible but more vulnerable to hacks. Cold storage involves keeping cryptocurrencies offline to enhance security.

Q15: How do I choose a cryptocurrency to invest in?

When choosing a cryptocurrency to invest in, consider factors such as the project's use case, technology, team, market trends, community support, and historical performance. It's also advisable to diversify your portfolio and invest only what you can afford to lose.

Q16: What are the potential benefits of blockchain technology?

Blockchain technology offers several benefits, including increased transparency, enhanced security, reduced transaction costs, faster settlement times, and the ability to operate without intermediaries.

Q17: Can blockchain technology be used for applications outside of finance?

Yes, blockchain technology has applications in various sectors beyond finance, including supply chain management, healthcare, education, voting systems, and digital identity verification.

Q18: What is tokenization, and why is it important?

Tokenization is the process of converting ownership rights or assets into digital tokens that can be traded on a blockchain. It is important because it can improve liquidity, fractional ownership, and facilitate the transfer of assets.

Q19: What are decentralized applications (dApps)?

Decentralized applications (dApps) are applications that run on a blockchain network, rather than a centralized server. They are designed to be open-source, secure, and resistant to censorship.

Q20: How is blockchain technology regulated?

Regulation of blockchain technology varies by country and often focuses on aspects such as anti-money laundering (AML), know your customer (KYC) requirements, and consumer protection. Regulatory bodies are still working to create comprehensive frameworks that address the unique challenges posed by blockchain and cryptocurrency.

FINAL QUIZ

Key Points

- Comprehensive Questions Covering All Chapters
- Answer Key

FINAL QUIZ: COMPREHENSIVE QUESTIONS COVERING ALL CHAPTERS

1. What is blockchain technology?

    a) A centralized database controlled by a government

    b) A decentralized ledger that records transactions across multiple computers

    c) A digital currency controlled by banks

    d) A paper-based financial record system

2. What is the main purpose of a blockchain's consensus mechanism?

    a) To provide financial advice

    b) To ensure that all participants in the network agree on the validity of transactions

    c) To centralize control of the network

    d) To hide transaction details from the public

3. **What was the primary motivation behind the creation of Bitcoin?**
    a) To increase government control over currencies
    b) To create a decentralized currency free from central banks
    c) To replace all traditional forms of currency
    d) To develop new online banking systems

4. **What is the role of cryptography in blockchain?**
    a) To make transactions private and secure
    b) To remove the need for transaction records
    c) To centralize the network
    d) To eliminate the need for miners

5. **How does Proof of Work (PoW) differ from Proof of Stake (PoS)?**
    a) PoW consumes more energy than PoS
    b) PoS requires solving complex puzzles, while PoW does not
    c) PoW is faster and cheaper than PoS
    d) PoS eliminates the need for any validators

6. **What is Bitcoin halving?**
    a) The doubling of Bitcoin's value every four years
    b) A reduction in the reward for mining new Bitcoin blocks
    c) A fork in the Bitcoin blockchain
    d) The splitting of Bitcoin into multiple tokens

7. **How does a smart contract function in a blockchain network?**
    a) It provides financial advice
    b) It is a self-executing contract with the terms directly written into code
    c) It replaces lawyers in legal agreements
    d) It is a manual verification system for contracts

8. Which of the following is an example of a stablecoin?

   a) Bitcoin

   b) Ethereum

   c) Tether (USDT)

   d) Litecoin

9. How does a cold storage wallet differ from a hot storage wallet?

   a) Cold storage is online, while hot storage is offline

   b) Cold storage is for small amounts, and hot storage is for large amounts

   c) Cold storage is offline, while hot storage is connected to the internet

   d) Cold storage uses more energy than hot storage

10. What are Decentralized Autonomous Organizations (DAOs)?

    a) Organizations governed by smart contracts on a blockchain

    b) Centralized institutions that manage cryptocurrencies

    c) Legal entities governed by traditional laws

    d) Companies that issue digital tokens for fundraising

11. How does a multi-signature wallet enhance security?

    a) It automatically generates a private key for users

    b) It requires multiple signatures to authorize transactions

    c) It eliminates the need for public keys

    d) It stores cryptocurrencies on a physical device

12. **What are Layer 2 solutions?**

    a) Protocols built on top of existing blockchains to improve scalability and speed

    b) New blockchains replacing older ones

    c) Security features designed to prevent fraud

    d) Tools for creating new cryptocurrencies

13. **What is the primary advantage of stablecoins over other cryptocurrencies?**

    a) They are decentralized

    b) They are immune to hacking

    c) They have stable values pegged to traditional assets

    d) They do not require internet access

14. **What is the significance of Ethereum's smart contract functionality?**

    a) It allows Ethereum to be faster than Bitcoin

    b) It enables automation of transactions based on pre-defined conditions

    c) It increases Ethereum's transaction fees

    d) It creates new types of digital coins automatically

15. **What role does a blockchain oracle play in smart contracts?**

    a) It eliminates the need for external data

    b) It verifies the identity of blockchain users

    c) It feeds real-world data to smart contracts

    d) It increases the speed of transaction processing

16. **What is decentralized finance (DeFi)?**

    a) A financial system built on blockchain that removes intermediaries like banks

    b) A platform for traditional banking services

    c) A centralized financial exchange for trading cryptocurrencies

    d) A government-controlled financial system

17. **How does tokenization work in a blockchain?**

    a) It converts real-world assets into digital tokens that can be traded on the blockchain

    b) It eliminates the need for cryptocurrencies

    c) It transfers ownership of assets to a central authority

    d) It increases the volatility of digital currencies

18. **What is the primary benefit of using a Proof of Stake (PoS) consensus mechanism?**

    a) Increased energy consumption

    b) Faster transaction times and lower energy consumption

    c) Increased transaction fees

    d) Reduces the number of transactions processed

19. **How does sharding help improve blockchain scalability?**

    a) It splits data across multiple blockchains to increase transaction speed

    b) It creates new blockchains for each transaction

    c) It centralizes blockchain data

    d) It eliminates the need for consensus mechanisms

20. **What is the purpose of anti-money laundering (AML) regulations in cryptocurrency?**

    a) To increase transaction fees

    b) To prevent the use of cryptocurrency for illegal activities

    c) To eliminate decentralized exchanges

    d) To control the value of cryptocurrencies

21. **What are the advantages of Central Bank Digital Currencies (CBDCs)?**

    a) They eliminate the need for traditional currencies

    b) They are government-backed digital currencies providing efficiency and transparency

    c) They increase the volatility of the digital economy

    d) They are completely anonymous and untraceable

22. **What is the primary function of a digital wallet?**

    a) To store and manage digital currencies and assets

    b) To create new blockchains

    c) To provide real-time market data

    d) To control consensus mechanisms

23. **How can blockchain technology improve supply chain management?**

    a) By providing transparency and tracking goods from origin to consumer

    b) By eliminating the need for physical goods

    c) By reducing taxes on imports and exports

    d) By allowing governments to control global trade

24. **What is the role of blockchain in eradicating illegal activities in financial systems?**

    a) By increasing anonymity in transactions

    b) By providing transparency and traceability, making it harder for criminals to hide illicit activities

    c) By allowing transactions without regulatory oversight

    d) By removing all transaction fees

25. **What is a governance token in a Decentralized Autonomous Organization (DAO)?**

    a) A token used to buy products on a blockchain

    b) A token that grants holders voting rights in a DAO

    c) A token that guarantees profit for its holders

    d) A token used to enforce smart contracts

26. **What is Know Your Customer (KYC) in the context of cryptocurrency?**

    a) A process to verify the identity of users to comply with regulations

    b) A method for creating new tokens

    c) A system for tracking cryptocurrency prices

    d) A mechanism for storing digital assets

27. **What challenge does the concentration of token ownership in DAOs create?**

    a) It makes decision-making faster

    b) It centralizes governance power

    c) It increases transparency

    d) It increases the number of voters

28. **What is the purpose of a smart contract in the decentralized finance (DeFi) ecosystem?**

   a) To manually validate transactions

   b) To automate financial transactions based on pre-defined conditions

   c) To manage supply chains

   d) To eliminate cryptocurrency wallets

29. **How does quantum computing pose a threat to blockchain security?**

   a) It increases blockchain scalability

   b) It could break current cryptographic methods, making blockchains vulnerable

   c) It makes consensus mechanisms obsolete

   d) It enhances privacy on blockchains

30. **What is the role of Chainalysis in the crypto ecosystem?**

   a) To provide blockchain analytics and assist with tracking illegal activities like money laundering and fraud

   b) To create new cryptocurrencies

   c) To centralize blockchain governance

   d) To automate smart contracts

31. **Why is blockchain technology considered a trustless system?**

   a) It requires trust in central authorities

   b) It eliminates the need for intermediaries or trusted third parties to verify transactions

   c) It increases the number of intermediaries required

   d) It decreases transaction speeds

32. **What is programmable money?**

    a) Digital money that can execute transactions based on predefined conditions

    b) A cryptocurrency that fluctuates in value

    c) A central bank currency used for international trade

    d) A traditional banknote that can be digitized

33. **How do decentralized exchanges (DEXs) differ from centralized exchanges (CEXs)?**

    a) DEXs allow peer-to-peer trading without intermediaries, while CEXs are managed by companies or institutions

    b) DEXs have higher fees than CEXs

    c) DEXs eliminate the need for digital wallets

    d) DEXs are regulated by governments, while CEXs are not

34. **What is the primary purpose of blockchain oracles in decentralized applications?**

    a) To control the consensus mechanism

    b) To provide external data to smart contracts for accurate execution

    c) To replace cryptocurrencies in transactions

    d) To store private keys for users

35. **How does the concept of immutability in blockchain help secure data?**

    a) It allows users to edit and modify previous blocks

    b) Once data is written on the blockchain, it cannot be altered, ensuring data integrity

    c) It eliminates the need for encryption in transactions

    d) It requires consensus to delete transactions

36. **What is a key advantage of tokenization in real estate using blockchain?**

    a) It reduces the value of real estate properties

    b) It allows fractional ownership and easier transfer of property assets

    c) It makes the real estate market more volatile

    d) It increases the need for intermediaries in transactions

37. **How can artificial intelligence (AI) enhance blockchain analytics?**

    a) By replacing miners with AI-based validators

    b) By improving fraud detection and transaction analysis through big data processing

    c) By creating new cryptocurrencies

    d) By centralizing the decision-making process

38. **What is the purpose of a consensus mechanism in decentralized systems?**

    a) To centralize decision-making

    b) To validate and agree upon the state of the blockchain without a central authority

    c) To increase transaction speeds by removing nodes

    d) To replace traditional currency with digital money

39. **How does blockchain interoperability benefit decentralized systems?**

    a) It increases the value of all blockchains

    b) It allows different blockchain networks to communicate and exchange data seamlessly

    c) It eliminates the need for wallets

    d) It centralizes all transactions into one network

40. **What is the significance of privacy-preserving technologies like zero-knowledge proofs (ZKPs) in blockchain?**

    a) They allow for completely anonymous transactions

    b) They enable parties to verify information without revealing the actual data, ensuring privacy and security

    c) They increase transaction fees to prevent malicious activity

    d) They eliminate the need for encryption

41. **How does a decentralized autonomous organization (DAO) operate?**

    a) It is run by a centralized authority that makes decisions

    b) It is governed by smart contracts, with stakeholders voting on key decisions

    c) It automatically creates new cryptocurrencies

    d) It replaces all traditional governance systems

42. **How does blockchain enhance cross-border payments?**

    a) By eliminating the need for smart contracts

    b) By reducing fees and processing times through decentralized systems

    c) By centralizing all transactions

    d) By replacing all forms of digital wallets

43. **What is the primary function of blockchain analytics companies like Chainalysis?**

    a) To centralize cryptocurrency exchanges

    b) To track and investigate suspicious transactions and illegal activities on the blockchain

    c) To create new consensus mechanisms

    d) To manage and control the issuance of new tokens

44. What is a key advantage of decentralized finance (DeFi)?

a) It eliminates the need for digital wallets

b) It allows peer-to-peer financial transactions without intermediaries like banks

c) It increases transaction fees to control volatility

d) It centralizes the control of financial systems

45. What is the role of quantum-resistant cryptography in blockchain?

a) It reduces the cost of mining

b) It protects blockchain systems from potential threats posed by quantum computing

c) It eliminates the need for consensus mechanisms

d) It centralizes blockchain data for faster processing

46. What is the primary purpose of a decentralized exchange (DEX)?

a) To allow direct peer-to-peer cryptocurrency trading without a central intermediary

b) To eliminate smart contracts from the blockchain

c) To centralize all transactions in a single network

d) To provide government-regulated trading platforms

47. What role do smart contracts play in automating financial transactions?

a) They allow users to manually approve every transaction

b) They self-execute financial transactions based on pre-set conditions without intermediaries

c) They increase transaction fees for faster execution

d) They centralize decision-making on the blockchain

48. **How does blockchain technology support supply chain transparency?**

    a) By hiding transaction details from all participants

    b) By allowing all participants to view the history of transactions and goods movement in real-time

    c) By increasing the need for intermediaries

    d) By removing the need for digital wallets

49. **What is the significance of AI-powered oracles in blockchain?**

    a) They control the issuance of new tokens

    b) They provide real-time, accurate external data to smart contracts for better decision-making

    c) They centralize the governance of decentralized networks

    d) They replace all miners in a blockchain network

50. **How does blockchain help mitigate the risks of money laundering and terrorism financing?**

    a) By making all transactions anonymous

    b) By providing transparency and traceability, making it easier to track illegal activities

    c) By increasing transaction fees to deter criminals

    d) By centralizing all financial transactions

☑ ANSWER KEY

1. b	18. b	35. b
2. b	19. a	36. b
3. b	20. b	37. b
4. a	21. b	38. b
5. a	22. a	39. b
6. b	23. a	40. b
7. b	24. b	41. b
8. c	25. b	42. b
9. c	26. a	43. b
10. a	27. b	44. b
11. b	28. b	45. b
12. a	29. b	46. a
13. c	30. a	47. b
14. b	31. b	48. b
15. c	32. a	49. b
16. a	33. a	50. b
17. a	34. b	

This final quiz covers a wide range of topics from the chapters and tests a broad understanding of blockchain, cryptocurrency, and related technologies.

REFERENCES

Chapter 1: Introduction to Blockchain Technology

- Nakamoto, S. (2008). *Bitcoin: A peer-to-peer electronic cash system*. https://bitcoin.org/bitcoin.pdf
- Tapscott, D., & Tapscott, A. (2016). *Blockchain revolution: How the technology behind Bitcoin is changing money, business, and the world*. Penguin.
- Swan, M. (2015). *Blockchain: Blueprint for a new economy*. O'Reilly Media.

Chapter 2: The History and Evolution of Cryptocurrency

- Antonopoulos, A. M. (2014). *Mastering Bitcoin: Unlocking digital cryptocurrencies*. O'Reilly Media.
- Narayanan, A., Bonneau, J., Felten, E., Miller, A., & Goldfeder, S. (2016). *Bitcoin and cryptocurrency technologies: A comprehensive introduction*. Princeton University Press.

Chapter 3: Key Cryptographic Concepts

- Stinson, D. R., & Paterson, M. B. (2018). *Cryptography: Theory and practice* (4th ed.). CRC Press.
- Schneier, B. (2015). *Applied cryptography: Protocols, algorithms, and source code in C* (20th anniversary ed.). John Wiley & Sons.

Chapter 4: Consensus Mechanisms in Blockchain

- Buterin, V. (2013). *A next-generation smart contract and decentralized application platform*. Ethereum White Paper. https://ethereum.org/en/whitepaper/

- Dwork, C., & Naor, M. (1992). *Pricing via processing or combatting junk mail.* In Proceedings of the 12th Annual International Cryptology Conference on Advances in Cryptology (pp. 139–147). Springer.

Chapter 5: Decentralized Finance (DeFi)

- Schär, F. (2021). *Decentralized finance: On blockchain- and smart contract-based financial markets.* Federal Reserve Bank of St. Louis Review, 103(2), 153–174. https://doi.org/10.20955/r.103.153-74
- Zhang, F., Zhou, J., & Zhang, X. (2020). *The role of decentralized finance in financial inclusion: A conceptual framework.* Journal of Financial Innovation, 6(1), 45–63.

Chapter 6: Smart Contracts and Their Applications

- Szabo, N. (1996). *Smart contracts: Building blocks for digital markets.* https://www.fon.hum.uva.nl/rob/Courses/InformationInSpeech/CDROM/Literature/LOTwinterschool2006/szabo.best.vwh.net/smart_contracts_2.html
- Christidis, K., & Devetsikiotis, M. (2016). *Blockchains and smart contracts for the internet of things.* IEEE Access, 4, 2292–2303.

Chapter 7: Central Bank Digital Currencies (CBDCs)

- BIS. (2020). *Central bank digital currencies: Foundational principles and core features.* Bank for International Settlements. https://www.bis.org/publ/othp33.pdf
- Kumhof, M., & Noone, C. (2018). *Central bank digital currencies—Design principles and balance sheet implications.* Bank of England.

Chapter 8: International Regulatory Approaches

- Zohar, A. (2015). *Bitcoin: Under the hood.* Communications of the ACM, 58(9), 104–113.
- Houben, R., & Snyers, A. (2018). *Cryptocurrencies and blockchain: Legal context and implications for financial crime, money laundering, and tax evasion.* European Parliament.

Chapter 9: Security and Risk Management in Blockchain

- Bonneau, J., Miller, A., Clark, J., Narayanan, A., Kroll, J. A., & Felten, E. W. (2015). *SoK: Research perspectives and challenges for Bitcoin and cryptocurrencies.* In Proceedings of the IEEE Symposium on Security and Privacy (pp. 104–121). https://doi.org/10.1109/SP.2015.14

Chapter 10: Crypto and Blockchain Adoption: A Global Perspective

- Hileman, G., & Rauchs, M. (2017). *Global blockchain benchmarking study.* Cambridge Centre for Alternative Finance. https://www.jbs.cam.ac.uk/faculty-research/centres/alternative-finance/publications/global-cryptocurrency-benchmarking-study/

Chapter 11: Blockchain in Supply Chain Management

- Kshetri, N. (2018). *Blockchain's roles in meeting key supply chain management objectives.* International Journal of Information Management, 39, 80–89.

Chapter 12: Blockchain in Education

- Grech, A., & Camilleri, A. F. (2017). *Blockchain in education.* Joint Research Centre (JRC) Technical Reports, European Commission. https://doi.org/10.2760/60649

Chapter 13: The Future of Money

- Yermack, D. (2017). *Corporate governance and blockchains.* Review of Finance, 21(1), 7–31. https://doi.org/10.1093/rof/rfw074

Chapter 14: Crypto, AI, and Blockchain

- Buterin, V. (2017). *The future of AI and blockchain: Can these two technologies work together?* https://blog.ethereum.org

Chapter 15: Decentralized Governance: Blockchain and the Future of Organizations

- Wright, A., & De Filippi, P. (2015). *Decentralized blockchain technology and the rise of lex cryptographia.* https://ssrn.com/abstract=2580664

Chapter 16: Conclusion: Embracing Change in the Financial World

- Swan, M. (2015). *Blockchain: Blueprint for a new economy.* O'Reilly Media.

Chapter 17: Appendices: Expert Interviews and Thought Leadership

- Hileman, G., & Rauchs, M. (2017). *Global blockchain benchmarking study.* Cambridge Centre for Alternative Finance. https://www.jbs.cam.ac.uk/faculty-research/centres/alternative-finance/publications/global-cryptocurrency-benchmarking-study/
- Mougayar, W. (2016). *The business blockchain: Promise, practice, and the application of the next internet technology.* Wiley.

Chapter 18: Final Quiz and Comprehensive Questions

- Narayanan, A., Bonneau, J., Felten, E., Miller, A., & Goldfeder, S. (2016). *Bitcoin and cryptocurrency technologies: A comprehensive introduction.* Princeton University Press.
- Antonopoulos, A. M. (2014). *Mastering Bitcoin: Unlocking digital cryptocurrencies.* O'Reilly Media.

www.ingramcontent.com/pod-product-compliance
Lightning Source LLC
Chambersburg PA
CBHW071710120626
46550CB00001B/172